CHILD OF OUR TIME:
EARLY LEARNING

D0064398

www.**rbooks**.co.uk

Also by Dr Tessa Livingstone:

Child of Our Time:
How to achieve the best for your child from conception to five years

CHILD OF OUR TIME:
EARLY LEARNING

Dr Tessa Livingstone

BANTAM PRESS

LONDON · TORONTO · SYDNEY · AUCKLAND · JOHANNESBURG

To the *Child of Our Time* families, for their
enthusiasm, generosity and affection.
To the BBC and the *Child of Our Time* team,
who have made the project fly.
And to Zoë and Charlie Jewell, loved
beyond measure.

TRANSWORLD PUBLISHERS
61–63 Uxbridge Road, London W5 5SA
A Random House Group Company
www.rbooks.co.uk

First published in Great Britain
in 2008 by Bantam Press
an imprint of Transworld Publishers

A CIP catalogue record for this book
is available from the British Library.

ISBN 9780593059272

Addresses for Random House Group Ltd companies outside the UK
can be found at: www.randomhouse.co.uk
The Random House Group Ltd Reg. No. 954009

The Random House Group Ltd makes every effort to ensure that the papers
used in its books are made from trees that have been legally sourced from
well-managed and credibly certified forests. Our paper procurement policy can
be found at: www.randomhouse.co.uk/paper.htm

Typeset in Garamond and DIN

Printed and bound in Germany

10 9 8 7 6 5 4 3 2 1

Every effort has been made to obtain the necessary permissions with reference to
copyright material, both illustrative and quoted. We apologize for any omissions in this
respect and will be pleased to make the appropriate acknowledgements
in any future edition.

CONTENTS

INTRODUCTION

Child of Our Time: Early Learning is the result of the fascination
with childhood I have had for many years, coupled with the unique
privilege of running an extraordinary twenty-year television project
called *Child of Our Time*. *Child of Our Time* is a vivid portrayal of
the lives of twenty-two families and explores the influences – genes,
upbringing, peers and society – that make us who we are. This huge
project has generated a detailed repository of research and experiments, backed by interviews and film of the families as they go about
their days. Its richness has been inspirational and is the impetus for
this book, which will reveal how your child changes from a baby
who knows very little to someone who has learnt enough to tackle
the world and win.

What makes us intelligent, resourceful, creative and flexible? Our
minds are the powerhouse for everything we think and do, but they
are all different, shaped not just by the genes we inherit but, crucially, by the knowledge, skills and attitudes we gain when we are
very young.

At the very beginning, newborn babies are ready and eager to
learn. But by the time our children start school, five years later, many
will have lost their all-embracing excitement for learning and be un-
willing to extend their skills to best advantage. So what can we do
to hone our children's skills? How can we improve their motivation,
concentration and intelligence? How do we all learn to remember?
And to read, do maths, enjoy art and music? How do our personal
styles of learning help or hinder us? How do our feelings affect what
or whether we learn? And how can we help our children make the
challenging transition from home to school?

Learning has always been essential, but it now seems more complicated than it has ever been. We live in a society which demands
immense flexibility and higher qualifications than ever, and where
the skills we learn today will not necessarily be enough to support
us tomorrow. The speed and level of information processing, inten-
sity of competition and frequency of decision-making are all increasing (think of the number of choices we have to make just to buy a
toothbrush!). To cope with this rapid change, we need to equip our
children with more than many of us have needed in the past – the
capacity and confidence to live a life of continuous and enthusiastic
learning.

Just as an active brain in an adult is the best guard against the ravages of old age, so an active brain in a child is the best guarantee of future intelligence. This book shows how we can encourage our children to learn a multiplicity of skills that will help them excel in learning, thinking and remembering. It begins by examining the amazing processes by which newborn babies learn, and ends with the adventure of school, during which time your child will have developed all the main skills for learning and know how to use them. This book shows how these vital skills develop – and is essential reading for parents and anyone who looks after children.

Child of Our Time: Early Learning is organized thematically into five parts.

PART ONE: **HOW TO LEARN**

Starting with newborn babies, who have very little knowledge but important latent skills, we find out about the basic techniques children need to master if they are to learn effectively: imitation, trial and error, association, language, deduction and induction. Using these skills, your child will learn to love learning.

PART TWO: **GET MOTIVATED!**

Motivation is the spur that makes us do things. Self-belief, resilience, concentration and the tactical use of rewards make our children keen to learn and able to adapt to new experiences. But how can we help them enjoy things that are difficult? And how does stretching our mind increase our intelligence?

PART THREE: **REMEMBER?**

Memory is the brain's most complex trick. We can hold and retrieve as much information as we want, if only we know how. We learn to remember by using our senses and by focusing and repeating, helped by some mnemonic ploys. But there's more to it than that. This section shows why we learn some things easily and forget others, and how we sometimes believe memories that are false.

PART FOUR: **THINK!**

Children think differently from adults for good reason. Children are supreme logicians, but don't yet know the facts of life so their deductions are frequently funny. This section will show you how to see through the mistakes children make to the brilliant strategy behind them, how they create their own universe using language, maths, art, music and creativity, and how thinking can boost both intelligence and happiness.

PART FIVE: RULES FOR SCHOOL

Children spend a vast part of their life in a rigid institution that will educate, inspire and sometimes irritate. It's school and it's important. So how can you find the right one? Why do children need to be prepared for the culture in schools? And what can you do to enable your child to discover the riches it can offer, while not being fazed by the difficulties?

This book has a strong practical bent, where theory generates suggestions for action, backed up by examples from the *Child of Our Time* project. Each chapter contains fun activities for children spanning the ages from birth to five and there are even some for parents. There are **fascinating facts** about behaviour. **Do It Yourself** gives you the opportunity to see how your and your child's mind works, and **A Day in the Lab** relates experiments that will surprise and amuse you. The book also contains timely contributions from the *Child of Our Time* families and many other people, who, by sharing their personal experiences, struggles, failures and victories, shed a unique light on problems your child may encounter in the real world. The gender issue – whether to refer to a generic child as 'he' or 'she' – has been solved the only way that seemed fair, by alternating the personal pronoun from chapter to chapter.

The book draws on the latest research in psychology, neuroscience, genetics and sociology to find learning strategies to fit every child's personality. It shows how you can use play to enhance your children's skills, when to leave them to discover on their own, and how to help children be motivated and resilient in the face of high expectations and their own vulnerability.

I hope you will learn a lot from this book, but, first – *how* will you learn it?

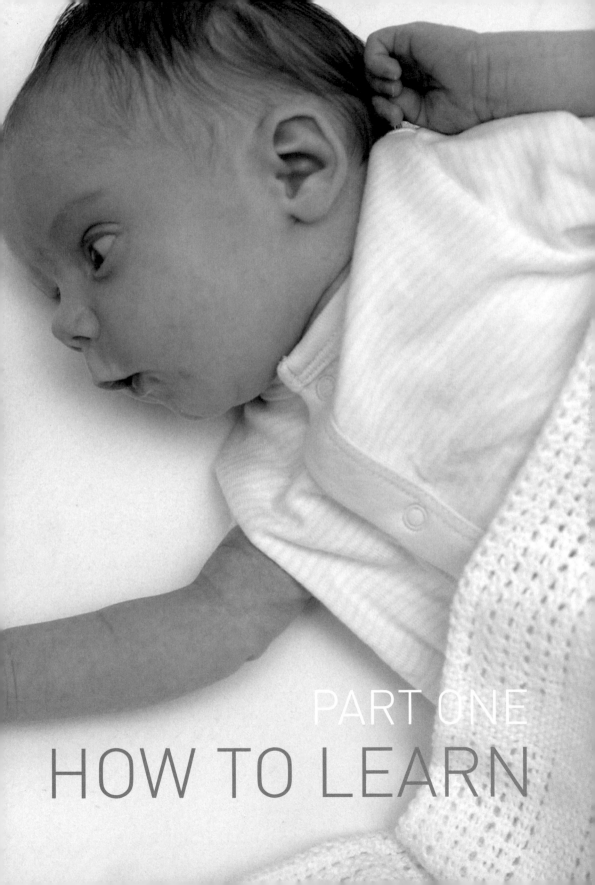

PART ONE
HOW TO LEARN

Teach your child to be passionate about learning and she will love to learn for the rest of her life.

HELENA'S STORY

Eight years ago I met a remarkable family. Barry and Jeanette Young joined up for our twenty-year-long BBC TV project, *Child of Our Time*, when Jeanette was pregnant with triplets, due in January 2000. A year later, they travelled from their home in the country to London with the BBC team for some special filming, bringing with them their small daughter, Helena.

Helena's story so far had been a tragic one. The triplets had been conceived by fertility treatment and at first everything had gone well, but just twenty-two weeks into her pregnancy Jeanette was rushed to hospital, and her first baby was born tragically early. They called him 'Little Barry', after his father. He was tiny, weighing just 1.2 kilos, his lungs too undeveloped to breathe, and he died after a few hours. Two weeks later, their second child, Millie, arrived. She too was very vulnerable, and could not sustain life outside the womb. Then came Helena, their third child. She survived – just – but she was very unwell. Her doctors, worried that her brain was badly damaged, suggested it might be best if her life support was switched off and she was allowed to die. It was a frightening prospect, but Barry and Jeanette had no doubts. They wanted their baby to live. For weeks, they sat with her in the special-care baby unit, talking to her, loving her, and living in hope.

Incredibly, tiny Helena pulled through, and after a gruelling five months in hospital she finally came home, with an oxygen cylinder to help her breathe and a very uncertain future. Her doctors warned her parents that she was guaranteed to have major problems.

It took a year for Helena to be well enough to live without extra oxygen, and even then she was virtually a prisoner in her own home, protected from any infection, however minor. Even a cold could have killed her. By now, Jeanette was managing the family business running children's care homes, but Barry was semi-retired and able to spend time with Helena, playing with her in their heated swimming pool, talking and reading to her, and giving her as many new experiences as possible. Even so, she was slow to develop and the family were, unsurprisingly, still very nervous. And then, eighteen months after her birth, she came to London to find out whether her brain was as damaged as her doctors had feared.

I was there with Helena when she had her extraordinary test. She was positioned inside a huge magnetic tube and looked very small and fragile when we left the room before the MRI scanner was activated. It was an agonizing wait, as pictures of her brain gradually formed on the screens in front of us. But as the minutes stretched out we began to realize that her brain didn't have any obvious defects, it looked much like any other child's. All the pictures we saw, before Helena woke up, were fine. The doctors hadn't found anything wrong with her.

What happened over the next two years was nothing short of miraculous. Though Helena was not even crawling at eighteen months, and was two before she spoke her first word, she eventually learnt to walk, run and talk. Now seven years old, she is a happy child, expressive, intellectually advanced and confident, and she has proudly started school, swamped by her new school uniform and loving it all. In 2004 Jeanette had another baby, again by IVF, Bella, a healthy little sister for Helena.

So how did little Helena get to be so smart? Many years ago, I started on a mission to find out how we learn in the early years of life. It's a wonderful process, but it's certainly not rocket science. Helena's parents stimulated her with all sorts of activities – physical, intellectual and sensory – because they trusted that she could learn. I came to the conclusion that every child has a brain that is a gargantuan learning machine, and what parents, friends, siblings and teachers need to do is to help each child recognize that she can use it, brilliantly.

So how do you start?

Begin at the Beginning

Your newborn baby is as hungry for knowledge as she is for food, and just as food shapes her body, experience shapes her brain.

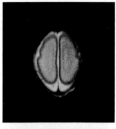
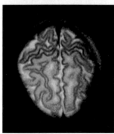

Fascinating facts about your child's brain
- It is the most complex structure in the known universe.
- All of us have a brain that transforms itself every minute of every day of our life.
- Half a million brain cells can be manufactured in a single minute.
- More than a billion connections between brain cells are made every day.
- Your child's brain has to work at least ten times harder than yours because her thinking isn't streamlined.
- Her brain learns more in the first three years of life than at any other time.
- Every experience changes your child's brain.

Your baby will learn because she must and because she is living in a world that excites her. To get her going, nature has provided her with a ready-made toolkit of nine mind-enhancing skills: looking, hearing, smelling, touching, tasting, moving, making noises, feeling emotions and curiosity. The role of parents is to help children use this toolkit to its best possible advantage.

This premature baby's brain, at twenty-four weeks (top left), looks very simple. A full-term baby's brain (below) is considerably more complex.

YOUR BABY HAS A REMARKABLE TOOLKIT OF SKILLS
- **Looking**: because she is fascinated by the beauty of the world. She especially likes looking at edges to learn the nature of objects.
- **Hearing**: because she loves to find out what noises mean and copy them.
- **Smelling**: because she needs to know when familiar things are near and she is safe.
- **Touching**: because she loves to feel things, and because touching helps her develop dexterity.
- **Tasting**: because she needs to learn to love the good food you give her, and hate anything bad.

- **Moving**: because she makes things happen; she turns her head to look at anything that moves because she's interested.
- **Making noises**: because she can tell you what she's thinking.
- **Feeling emotions**: because they allow her to know herself; if things get too much, she will switch off.
- **Curiosity**: because it drives her to learn more about her wonderful world.

She will learn faster if you help her exploit the skills she's born with.

In order to activate the essential skills that nature has provided for your baby, she needs to be excited and stimulated by the world from a very early age. At birth your baby doesn't know the basics. It's hard to imagine, but she doesn't know what an object is or whether it will stay put or disappear when she glances away. She knows very few facts and remembers very little. She even has to learn who you are. But what she does have is an unconquerable thirst for knowledge, and one of the first things she concentrates on is people's faces. Individual faces are incredibly important to babies, who depend on a special someone to look after them. So learning what a face is and who it belongs to is a top priority. Learning to recognize the faces of those she sees regularly can happen quite fast, but realizing that someone is a stranger takes a surprisingly long time, as I could see when I spent some time observing my friend's newborn baby, Elisha.

ELISHA'S STORY

I first visited Elisha just after she was born. She could only focus on something about an arm's length away – the distance of my face as I cradled her in my arms. Elisha seemed to know that faces are important and she locked eyes with me. But did she know me? There is evidence that newborns will gaze at two dots above one dot just as happily as at a parent, and sure enough, when I showed her some dots she locked eyes with them too. There was another classic moment a few days later when she started to stare at my hairline. Her eyes followed the movements of my head and sometimes darted from one side of my face to the other. I felt, with some wonder, that I was watching her computing the shape of my face and its boundaries. By the time of my next visit she was much more sociable. But although it was clear that she knew her mum's face very well, she smiled charmingly and indiscriminately at everyone else. It wasn't until she was three months old that she started to find me scary, showing that she could now recognize the face of a relative stranger.

A fascinating fact about hearing

Most of us naturally talk to babies in a high-pitched voice, and until I did some research I didn't know why. The answer is simple. Babies hear best in the high-frequency range and that's because a tiny bone in the inner ear that carries bass tones to the eardrum and the brain isn't in place at birth. Why? Because the strong sound of the mother's heartbeat would be deafening inside the womb. It takes several months for deep noises, like grandad's bass grumble, to be audible. So when we talk to babies in the high babyish voice called 'motherese' we are, unthinkingly, giving our babies what they need.

WHAT YOU CAN DO ... for young children

- Observe your baby and find out how she responds to the things she sees, touches, smells and hears. It will give you an insight into her emerging character and help you to tailor what you do to what she needs.
- You will see that your baby is fascinated with boundaries and movement as she works out how to identify the many objects around her. Try hanging a black and white patterned mobile out of reach but in the line of sight, or fix a safety mirror firmly to her cot – your baby will be intrigued by the mobile little face she sees, and will try to touch it, though she won't yet recognize it. This will stimulate her curiosity and encourage her to reach out, and watching the changing view will feed her love of novelty.

A fascinating fact about crying

Babies have an extremely loud cry for their size; it is the equivalent of you or me making as much noise as a pneumatic drill. The volume of their cries could be one reason babies are born with weaker hearing than adults; if their hearing was acute they would deafen themselves.

- Your baby listens to all the sounds around her. Speak to her, encourage her to mimic the noises you hear, show her where they come from – a car on the road outside, a bird in a tree – and sing with her.

A fascinating fact about your child's first words

Babies try to talk when they are very young, as I found out when I heard one of my children murmuring, cooing and giggling to herself in her cot and went to sit silently by her open door to listen. Gradually I realized she was doing something magical: she was inventing a language and trying it out in the empty room. She was remarkably careful, repeating her nonsense words alone and in combination with other 'words'. This charming moment was her first attempt to speak and marked the start of her long journey to fluency. If I could put that noise in a tin, I would, and keep it for times when I feel a little doleful. An amazing experience, and one I shall never forget.

- Give your child gentle massages – it will make her feel safe and releases a rush of feel-good hormones. Touch has immense power; it can help premature babies to put on weight more quickly and contributes to longevity in adults, because it is one of the most potent ways to communicate love.
- Your baby can recognize people by their smell when her eyes are still struggling to focus. Smells are powerful; they lodge in the unconscious and generate memories. A comfort blanket or soft toy that hasn't been washed has a smell that your child will connect with feelings of drowsy happiness, so precious possessions must be washed with care. Even a new book has its own scent which, if you and your child enjoy reading together, will forever trigger feelings of pleasure and excitement.
- Try to stimulate all her senses with toys that make a noise when you squeeze them, or have twinkling lights that pander to her love of novelty. Encourage her to grab, look, hear and make noises and let her play alongside children's TV with its songs, rhymes, movement and vivid colours.
- Your baby already understands some emotions. Help her learn more by letting her see your facial expressions, exaggerate them and name them. Name her emotions too, she needs to recognize what she feels.
- Smile at your baby, laugh with her – the feel-good hormones this produces will make you both very happy.

Babies learn the shape of your face and hair and use them as cues to recognize you. Try putting a hat on and see if your baby knows who you are or is baffled! There is a short window of time, around a few weeks old, when your baby will not recognize you unless she can see your hairline.

A fascinating fact about interpreting facial expressions

Even the tiniest babies are born with the ability to understand the main emotions, and to express them, but it can take at least sixteen years to understand more complex facial expressions like curiosity or nervous anticipation.

Your baby will change remarkably quickly, both physically and mentally. She will be infected by your enthusiasm, and as you build up a repertoire of games you both enjoy – tickling, chatting, singing, holding her high in the air, sloshing water over her tummy – you will notice an equal pleasure in predictability and novelty, and a gradual shift from gentle interaction to rougher, more daring games. It is essential to encourage her to extend her boundaries when she is ready, keeping her from boredom and helping her to become adventurous; this will benefit her both intellectually and socially.

So what techniques do children use to learn everything they need to know? And why? In the next five chapters we will look at how you can harness the four fundamental ways we learn: by association, imitation, exploration and rote learning. But first, I'm going to explore your child's unique style of learning. Find out how you can maximize her personal potential to learn anything, anytime, anywhere.

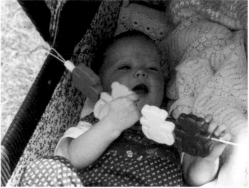

Learning Styles

Your child is unique. There will never be anyone with his brain, his potential or his desires. No one else in the world will ever think like him.

Because your child is unique, the way he learns will also be unique. He will learn using all his senses and many different pathways through his brain. Some things will come more naturally than others, depending on what he enjoys, what he finds difficult and which of the many learning methods suit his particular personality. Some people learn well by looking and visualization, some like to speak and listen, others say they learn when they do something active. Some of us learn best alone, others in groups. We may be logical, working our way up to big ideas from first principles, or we may start with a big intuitive idea and dig down for evidence. These seven learning styles can be used in any combination, but there is an assumption that we tend to have a preference for just one or two of them.

A fascinating fact about our learning styles

One fun way of divining people's preferred style is to listen to what they say. People with a visual style seem to have a tendency to use words like 'Look at how this works for you' or 'I can't quite picture that.' Those of us who prefer the auditory style are apparently more prone to say 'That sounds about right' or 'I hear you'. Kinaesthetic and tactile people might use phrases like 'That feels right' or 'My guts tell me that …'

The most commonly used learning styles are visual, auditory and kinaesthetic/physical, reflecting how we use our senses to inform thinking and memory. Some people remember pictures very well, while others use – and memorize – words. Still others have a strong sense of kinaesthesia, which gives them a physical intelligence that makes it easier to learn new skills like climbing or building, and mediates memories via actions. Although everyone uses all their senses, we usually find that one predominates. Before you think about your children's favourite styles, it is worth finding out about yourself.

DO IT YOURSELF

Are you a visual learner? An auditory learner? Or a kinaesthetic/physical learner? Find out with this **Adult Sensory Learning Styles Questionnaire.**

When you ...	Visual	Auditory	Physical/Kinaesthetic
Spell	Do you try and see the word?	Do you sound out the word or use a phonetic approach?	Do you write the word down to find out if it feels right?
Talk	Do you talk sparingly and dislike listening for too long? Do you favour words such as 'see', 'picture' and 'imagine'?	Do you enjoy listening and are impatient to talk? Do you use words such as 'hear', 'tune' and 'think'?	Do you gesture and use expressive movements? Do you use words such as 'feel', 'touch' and 'hold'?
Concentrate	Are you distracted by untidiness or movement?	Are you distracted by sound or noises?	Are you distracted by activity around you?
Meet someone again	Do you forget names, but remember faces or where you met?	Do you forget faces, but remember names or remember what you talked about?	Do you remember best what you did together?
Contact people on business	Do you prefer direct face-to-face meetings?	Do you prefer the telephone?	Do you like to talk with them while walking or participating in an activity?
Read	Do you like descriptive scenes or pause to imagine the actions?	Do you enjoy dialogue and conversation or 'hear' the characters talk?	Do you prefer action stories or are not a keen reader?
Do something new at work	Do you like to see demonstrations, diagrams, slides or posters?	Do you prefer verbal instructions or talking about it with some-one else?	Do you prefer to jump right in and try it?
Put something together	Do you examine the diagrams and pictures?	Do you read the directions or ask someone?	Do you ignore the directions and figure it out as you go along?
Need help with a computer application	Do you seek out pictures or diagrams?	Do you call the help desk, ask a neighbour or growl at the computer?	Do you keep trying, or try it out on another computer?

You probably discovered that you use different learning styles, depending on the task, as I did when I did this learning-styles test. But most of us major in one – in my case, visualization. So, when I was on a quest to spell a difficult word, I started by visualizing the word; then, as I was still unsure, I went through the full gamut of possibilities, writing the word down and sounding it out. I asked a friend to do the same and she had a different pattern, starting with sounding it out, then writing and then looking at it. Young children take time to develop a clear learning style; even so, it is possible to explore theirs with them, and find out about their earliest predispositions.

DO IT YOURSELF

This learning-styles test is for children of around five or six, but you can try it with younger ones, as long as you make allowances for the slower development of verbal skills and tailor your questions to their level.

1 Ask your child to describe a journey in his day. It could be anything, from walking upstairs to going to the shops. This is a very visual task, so first ask yourself a few questions. Does it sound as if he is seeing the route? Does he say 'It looks like...' or 'I can see...'? Does he shut his eyes? And is it accurate and detailed? If it is, then he is likely to have a good visual imagination.

2 Read him a story without showing him the pictures and then ask him what he remembers. This is a verbal task. Does he listen intently, or say some of the words as you go along? After it has finished, does he repeat some of the story verbatim? Does he add verbal descriptions, elaborating on what he has heard? Is he accurate in his rendition of the story? If so, he is likely to major in the auditory style of learning.

3 Ask your child what physical activity he did today. This looks at kinaesthetic/physical/tactile memory. When he is describing his activity, does he show you all the actions? Does he gesticulate about it? Does he enthusiastically re-enact more than one of the day's activities? Does he use props? If so, he is likely to learn well by doing.

Your child may learn using all these three styles, but one of them is likely to come out on top. The most used style for children of this age is visual; physical/kinaesthetic comes next, then auditory. Try the test again in a year. Learning styles are adaptable and, as your child grows, his preferred learning style may evolve, especially if he has a parent or teacher who prefers one style above the others.

Sensory learning styles represent one type of learning, but psychologists have also looked at the differences between solitary learning and learning with other people, and how we grasp concepts, either intuitively, working down to find evidence, or logically, working up from the evidence. These approaches can be hard to identify definitively in young children, but when we asked parents in our longitudinal study, *Child of Our Time*, about their children, they knew precisely where their talents lay.

Child of Our Time parents speak

The *Child of Our Time* children were six years old when we discovered how much learning styles influenced what they do. These are just some of them …

Matthew is a *visual thinker*, and his mother Kathryn is very proud of him.

" Matthew has got a really good memory, to the point where it seems almost photographic, and he's very good at building things; he's very dextrous and he's careful when I give him jobs that are quite intricate. He's very good with his hands and brilliant at building Lego. "

Look at them

Rhianna is very good at talking and has always been happy to make up stories about what she sees. Like both her parents, she has an enormous vocabulary and seems to have a fabulous *auditory-vocal* way of learning. Tanya, her mother, finds her a good companion.

" Rhianna has liked to find out about words since she was very young, and she never lets a word go by that she doesn't understand. She picks up new information from television and works out connections between ideas, like why dinosaurs died out and crocodiles didn't. She's always been read to and picks out really difficult books. She was fascinated by Salvador Dali and wanted me to explain all about what the pictures and captions meant. And of course she has parents who never shut up. That helps! "

They've got pooey bottoms.

Why do sheep poo everywhere?

William is good at school work, but his favourite activity is sport and he learns quickly – he's a natural *kinaesthetic/physical* learner. Gillian, his mother, thinks he has real potential.

> " William is naturally good at sports; I think it's genetic because he's just like his father. He's got an amazing sense of balance and his hand-eye coordination is definitely natural. His absolutely favourite thing is sport. He's only seven, but he goes to tennis lessons after school and beats really good children three years older than him and then he comes home and wants to play cricket till all hours. He likes making things too. He made a lovely clay owl and he and his brother have made hundreds of paper aeroplanes and now they're all over the house. I'm sure he's talented enough to be the best tennis player, but I want him to have the opportunity to be an artist if he decides he wants it! "

Calvin is very *logical* and loves science. His mother Helen is very proud of his determination to experiment at any cost.

> " Calvin loves finding things out. We do a lot of science experiments, like we made Coca Cola explosions by putting bicarbonate of soda into the bottle – you have to jump back quickly or you get soaked! Calvin loves Planet Earth but we don't see much of the programmes because he asks too many questions. One day he found a dead pigeon. It looked quite nice so he took it to school for 'Show and Tell'! His teacher told him to take it out, but he'd already shown it to the other children in the playground, so it didn't matter. It sounds disgusting, but I would much rather he can be a real child, make messes and answer his own questions; he won't get away with dissecting dead pigeons when he's older! "

Ethan is very *intuitive*, and Kerri has seen his talent in action for many years.

> ❝ *Ethan doesn't learn like other kids, he sees things differently. He's very machine minded. Sometimes it takes him a while to find out how something works, and sometimes he goes the wrong way and I think 'What's he doing?', and then a few minutes later I say 'Huh, now I see it!' He's very confident within himself in some ways, and absolutely brilliant at computer games. He just seems to get what the whole thing's about.* ❞

Helena likes *learning alone*, getting wholly absorbed in made-up worlds. Her mother, Jeanette, thinks this could serve her well in the future.

> ❝ *Helena is very focused on what she's doing. She can blank out the rest of the world and you wouldn't know that she was there. She gets into her zone and that's it. I think she is very self-motivated. Though that's a grown-up word to put on a six-year-old!* ❞

Megan is very sociable and likes *learning with people*. Her mother Gaynor is quite jealous of her social skills!

> ❝ *Megan loves to play with other children and I can see that she's going to be very good at delegating. She's a good organizer, quite bossy in a nice way. She can work people out and get them to do things that I definitely wouldn't be able to do any day.* ❞

Since learning styles are all useful in their own way, the trick that would most benefit your child is to be able to use them all, singly or in combination. There is very good evidence that using all our senses allows us to learn much more effectively than if we use just one. To that end, there is training you can do to help your child master each learning style.

A DAY IN THE LAB

Last year we did an experiment with some of the *Child of Our Time* children, who were then five years old. It was simple: we taught our children Polish! We put out ten types of food – things like sweets, pineapple, cake and cheese – and told them the Polish names for those foods. Then we tested them. Most of the children learnt nothing. Just a few, the ones with the most retentive minds, remembered one or two words. So we tried again with another ten foods, but this time we allowed them to pick the food up, inspect it, talk about it and taste it. This time our children *did* learn; there was a fantastic 150 per cent improvement. That's because they were allowed to use not only visual and auditory learning styles, but also others, proving how effective it can be to use several learning styles at the same time.

Learning how to use each style will take time; your child won't learn them all for many years. But the following sections offer a variety of activities for young children. You will need to pick and choose the activities and reshape them so they are appropriate for your child's age and particular personality.

Visual Style

Encourage your child to do things that develop his powers of visualization: drawing, describing the walk to the shops or describing objects in detail. There is much to be gained by training him in visualization. By using his magical inner eye, he can visualize an activity he really wants to do, like running fast, writing a word neatly or throwing a ball – you'll be amazed how visualization increases the speed at which he learns.

A fascinating fact about visualization

Psychologists have discovered that visualizing can greatly assist us to learn new skills. The visualization must be as detailed as possible, starting from the first move – for instance, placing a football down on the ground if you are visualizing kicking – and going through the action in as much detail as possible, right to the very end. During this process the part of your brain that controls movement practises switching muscles on and off and the muscles twitch imperceptibly in response.

The amazing power of visualization can amplify not only our learning, but also our strength. One scientist, Dr Ranganathan, got his students to either flex their little finger by pressing it sideways against an immovable object or to visualize doing so. After three months' practice, the strength of the flexor muscles had increased by over 50 per cent in those who had made the movement, and by 35 per cent – not much less – if the movement had just been visualized. Mental training seemed to have strengthened the nerve signal to the finger so much that the muscle actually performed better. He was so interested in this result that he repeated the experiment with muscles in the elbow and the mental magic worked again.

Auditory Style

Try to persuade your child to tell stories, to write a play, to be very persuasive or to talk like a character on TV. You can teach him rhymes and challenge him with riddles and double meanings. Again, there is much to be gained by training him in auditory skills – he will gradually become fluent and so quick witted he'll make up rhymes and play games with his words.

Physical-Kinaesthetic-Tactile Style

Try learning by doing; for instance, finding out about the natural world through bird-spotting and gardening, learning stories through acting and maths through playing games, from peek-a-boo to pacing out distances. The value of this learning style lies in the bodily memory of skills learnt, the joy of movement and the positive effects of fitness on the brain.

Logical-Mathematical Style

This is also important, so promote this precise and detailed exploration of the world. It will become the basis for masterful thinking in the future! Do maths calculations with your child, encourage him to argue logically and help him work out how to solve problems and find the logical next step. Even babies learn to use logic – try hiding a toy and find out where he looks for it, or see how quickly he realizes when a ball, rolled on the ground, will reach his hand.

Intuitive Style

Talking about his ideas can fire your child's imagination, and you can help by discussing the wonders of the cosmos or the beauty of

a flower. Don't worry if it goes over his head, he can revel in the bigness of the universe or the smallness of an insect without really understanding the difference. Let him take the lead and don't inhibit his imagination by telling him his facts are wrong, rather encourage invention and a questioning attitude. The prize for being able to think intuitively lies in the capacity to see something as a whole, and to make wonderful creative leaps.

Social Style

To enhance your child's collaborative skills, all you have to do is to work cooperatively together, whether you are making noises or inventing stories. Indulge your child's passion for knowledge by going shopping together or visiting a museum. One, two or even ten brains working with him will open his mind and make for explosive leaps in learning!

Solitary Style

Most children of all ages like to play on their own at times. All they need is appropriate resources: toys, pens, paper, books, and space to spread. Learning alone offers an amazing reward – the mental state called 'flow' where you are so focused and single-minded that everything else disappears. Flow puts you in a good mood, generating joy.

Combining Learning Styles

There are many everyday tasks that use a range of styles, and intuitively we tend to start in one mode and add others. Try doing that with your child. For instance, take a common problem, such as finding a lost toy. Talk about where it might have gone, ask him to visualize where he last saw it, then go to that place and search. If it isn't there then there must be a logical reason. Has it been tidied away? Or has he forgotten when he actually did see it last? Once the toy is found you can go for the big idea – we all lose things and we can almost always find them – if we try hard enough!

SALLY'S STORY

Seven-year-old Sally had a wonderful imagination and was passionate about telling stories, but she relied heavily on her facility with language and liked to control her games to the point where she got angry when friends tried to join in. Her father was a convivial man who wanted his only daughter to be more receptive, so he suggested that they put on a play based on one of her favourite stories. Sally's older cousins came round to help, deciding to make colourful backdrops and to use the comedic talents of one and the musical flair of another. They shared out parts and revised the script. A week – and a lot of work – later, the new theatre group performed what turned out to be a wonderful show, applauded

enthusiastically by the whole family, and Sally, as author, was given special acclaim. This experience revealed a new world and the joys of working with her big cousins to make a visual spectacle opened her mind. And there was another bonus. It generated a new family tradition, an annual performance, which lasted for many years.

Learning-styles tests have become big business, used by schools and sold over the internet, and for good reason. With age and practice, we can learn to use all of the many diverse styles to help us. In comparison, our brain's underlying mechanisms that allow us to learn from the day of our birth are instinctive and universal; they are written into our DNA.

There are four mechanisms that we use to learn. All are equally valuable and are used by every human on the planet. The most well-known methods are imitation, exploration and rote learning, but the most awesome is less obvious. It is called 'learning by association'.

Learning by Association

3

Learning by association is probably your child's most formidable tool for learning. If two or more things happen together in time and space, then your child will make an association between them. The more emotional the experience and the more often it happens, the stronger the association. This learning occurs almost without you knowing.

Our brain is hard-wired to remember experiences that happen at roughly the same time and in the same place. This unconscious process is called 'learning by association'. For instance, if you drive to work every day through streets congested with traffic jams, you may well associate the journey with frustration and anger, and if you think about the journey afterwards you will feel those emotions again because your brain has made a strong link between the drive, the traffic jam and a bad mood. This type of learning is so fundamental that even fish, which have tiny brains, use it. If a small fish escapes from a predator it will associate fear with the predator, and when it next encounters the predator the fear will make the fish flee before an attack. Learning by association can save human lives, too. Children badly frightened by a near miss on the roads rarely walk out without looking again.

Learning by association is remarkable not least because, of all the learning tools, it is the earliest to develop. Even the youngest of babies is hard-wired to link things that happen together in time and space. Babies can even learn by association before they are born, a fact I discovered when we asked some enthusiastic mothers from our children's project *Child of Our Time* to play their favourite piece of music to their unborn babies. After the children were born, this piece of music, associated as it was with the comfort and safety of the womb, proved to be potent medicine. When the fractious babies listened to it they immediately calmed down!

One of the most fascinating things we learn by association is language. The word is spoken, the object seen, and the association happens. It's incredible how quickly your child can learn language through this unconscious process.

Tyrese in the lab with his mum, Marie.

A DAY IN THE LAB

I've witnessed an experiment where babies less than a year old were shown a series of pictures of strange objects at the same time as a voice said a nonsense word. The babies saw and listened and, much to my surprise, after only one showing, often looked straight at the correct object when its nonsense name was spoken. There is no known limit to the number of words your child's brain can absorb like this. Such innate intelligence is awe-inspiring and such capacity to learn humbling.

Think how many important things your child learns by association:
Facts like:
- Water comes from taps
- Cushions are soft
- Telephones ring.

Skills like:
- Language: objects, feelings and actions link with words
- Reading: the sound of the word links with its shape on a page
- Routes to places: what you see links with where you are.

Expectations like:
- Parents coming home from work link with excitement
- Getting in the car links with boredom
- Time with relatives links with having fun and games.

Routines like:
- Cleaning teeth links with going to bed
- Putting on a coat links with going outside
- Picking up a sibling from school links with not getting attention for a while.

Behaviour like:
- Joking links with being happy
- Watching TV links with being quiet
- Asking for help links with your loving attention.

Learning by association is often an unconscious process – it just happens. The great psychiatrist Sigmund Freud was the first to examine how much the unconscious learning of associations affects us and how unique our associations are. If you ask your friends to write down ten quick associations with the word 'home', you will find that everyone's list is different, resonating with their own particular experiences. These associations colour our feelings and influence our actions.

A DAY IN THE LAB

A child was taken into a room lightly scented with lavender and asked to do an easy task. She loved it, and the task was completed quickly. She was then taken into an identical room, scented with rose water. There she was faced with an impossible task, a puzzle that had no solution. It was very frustrating and she left feeling a failure. Some months later she came back, but this time both rooms contained a challenging but do-able new task. In the rose-scented room the girl burst into tears and failed. But the identical task in the lavender-scented room made her smile and she succeeded! Unconsciously she had connected the smell of lavender with success. This experiment has been repeated with many children. The results attest to the power of the unconscious associations we make between smells, emotions and actions.

The impact of this mechanism cannot be underestimated. Learning by association, your child is taught from the very beginning about his own worth. Feeling good about yourself is absolutely vital if you are to be enthusiastic about learning.

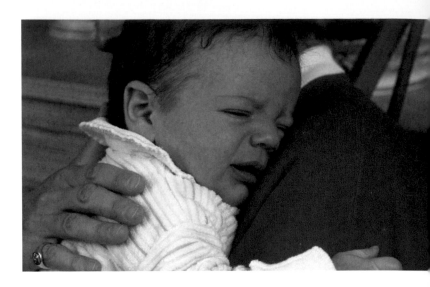

KARIM'S STORY

Janine had wanted a baby for years and when baby Karim arrived she was delighted. But things didn't go well from the start. Janine was a loving mother but couldn't handle Karim's crying, and cry he did. He had colds and colic and cried, it seemed, for no reason at all. And Janine couldn't bear it. Gradually she started to ignore his cries, blocking the noise and hoping it would go away. It never did. In fact it got worse, until Janine was at her wits' end. And then she did something brave: she recognized she had a problem and went to a child psychologist and begged for help. What she got were some very simple instructions. Every time Karim cried she was to drop what she was doing and comfort him. At first it was hard. Karim wasn't used to it and couldn't settle and Janine felt rejected and dispirited. But she stuck with it and very gradually Karim's crying grew less and he began to make other, nicer, cooing noises, the baby equivalent of 'Hi Mum,' telling Janine he needed her.

This slow transformation changed their lives. Early in life Karim had learnt by association that only the loudest, longest cries bring help, that life is an anxious business and, more scarily, that he wasn't really worth anyone's attention. Now Janine had taught him another lesson: to associate her not with neglect, but affection. It's this association that causes babies whose parents respond fast to cry less, while those who are left to be 'taught a lesson' learn the wrong one and cry more. How much better Janine and Karim felt about themselves and each other when they had learnt that they loved and were loved in return.

A fascinating fact about fear

There are some things we learn over a period of time, and others that are learnt in a single intense moment, usually because we have been very frightened. Most of us resist eating or drinking anything that has once made us sick and shy away from an activity that has harmed us. It's called 'one-trial learning'. One-trial learning can work positively too, a fact illustrated by the strange behaviour of newborn chicks. Newborn chicks are born knowing they must immediately find a protector, so in the single intense moment when they open their eyes they learn one thing – to follow the first object they see. Usually it is their mother. But not always. Sometimes it is a human being.

Because learning by association is completely automatic, it is often assumed that we do not need to know how to use it, but we do. This most powerful of tools can make our and our children's lives a lot easier, but only if we understand how it works.

JOE'S STORY

Last year I was with a couple who live in the country. Jane and Angus have three children and the youngest is a boy called Joe. He was then five years old and he'd spent the afternoon playing football with his friends. It was one of those damp, muddy autumn days and we were comfortably warm in the living room by the time an excited Joe erupted into the house, leapt on to the sofa and started telling us all about the goals he'd scored and the brilliant passes he'd made. But his parents weren't sharing his excitement. Before he was halfway through his story Jane was angrily removing his shoes, Angus was shouting at him, and splodges of mud were all over the sofa. Joe's face held an extraordinary mixture of emotions – fright, contrition and a sort of anger, as though the mess was his parents' fault.

By the time everything was cleared up, I had decided that he might be right to feel aggrieved; maybe this situation was partly his parents' fault. So I asked him about it, and he told me that he only remembered about his shoes when it was too late. With his parents' permission I took Joe to the back door and asked him to put his muddy shoes on and go outside to play for a few minutes. I shut the door and waited for him to come back. When he did I asked him what he should do; he told me, and took off his shoes. We did this little exercise five times, until he said he thought he would remember 'for ever and ever and ever!' But I wasn't so sure, so I suggested to Jane and Angus that they encourage him to visualize coming in the door, taking off his shoes and going into the house with his slippers on. From then on, Joe remembered.

So what had changed? When I first saw him smearing mud over the sofa he had already made strong associations between the need to take his shoes off and his parents' anger in the living room. It didn't occur to him to think of mud or shoes until he got to the place where retribution was delivered. All he needed was help to alter his associations and think of muddy shoes the moment he came into the house.

WHAT YOU CAN DO ... for all children

- A home full of love, acceptance and fun leads to the most positive associations for all happy families.
- Remember to involve as many senses and learning styles as possible if you want an association to stick. Your child can learn by practising an action, by seeing, by hearing, by understanding the big picture and by knowing the answers to detailed 'why' questions.
- Observe your child and see if you can tell what some of her associations might be. Do you feel good about them? If so, that's fine; if not, think about how to shift them.

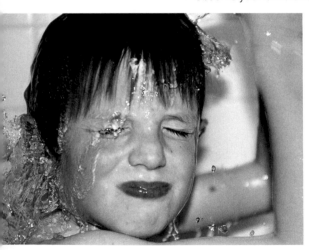

- Be consistent – if you want your child to associate your pleasure with doing something she and you enjoy, express your appreciation every time until the association becomes strong and solid.

WHAT YOU CAN DO ... for babies

- Encourage your baby to make associations by showing her the connection between words, events, actions and emotions, and show your appreciation when she gets it right.

- Some babies don't like baths. Is she afraid because of a scary one-trial learning moment? Let her have a bath with you. And some children always want to snuggle up on a particular cushion – maybe she associates it with the pleasure of watching a special TV programme or playing a favourite game.
- Keep it simple – if you want to teach your baby a new word, point out the object you are naming.

WHAT YOU CAN DO ... for toddlers

- Teach positive associations. For instance, if you think she might spill some juice, tell her that the juice stays in the cup, rather than saying 'Watch out, you'll spill it!' The former will make her visualize being careful and she will be; the latter presents her with a picture of the drink dropping to the floor, which makes it much more likely to happen!
- Look out for one-trial learning. The effects of a really nasty experience like being barked at by an aggressive dog or eating something that makes her sick could last for a long time. Your child is sensible, however, and even if the association is deeply embedded she will be able to change the association with your help, if you are clear, consistent and patient.

WHAT YOU CAN DO ... for older children

- Teach associations in the right place. So if you want your child to take her shoes off at the front door, rehearse the task right there. Locations are often important for adults too – how often do we go to a room to get something, forget what it is and, embarrassingly, have to go back to the place we first thought of it to remember?
- Actions speak louder than words – so if you want to help your child associate reading with pleasure, enjoy a book with her, and if you want your child to go to sleep happily then teach good habits by keeping bedtime regular, quiet and cosy.
- Association games can be fun. For instance, try asking your child to associate freely around a word or a story, coming up with words or ideas that she connects with the subject. The results may tell you a lot about her vivid imagination and beliefs. Kids link all sorts of surprising things together and can come out with remarkably interesting stories.

Imitation

Your child is born able to copy others and long may it last. Copycats learn from the masters. Copycats have a head start. Copycats are successful.

When my daughter was just a day old, a friend of mine came round and put her tongue out at my lovely newborn baby, and something amazing happened. My daughter stuck her tongue out too!

Imitating others is one of the fastest and most effective ways of learning, which is odd because, when you think about it, copying isn't simple at all. It requires some real joined-up thinking, connecting someone else's action, which you can see but not feel, with your own movement, which you can feel but not see.

A DAY IN THE LAB

The brain of a small fish is 3,000 times smaller than that of a human, and some people believe that fish can only remember things for three seconds, but is this true? Surprisingly, the basic process of learning is the same in fish as in humans, as I found out when I went to see a researcher who made a film for ignorant fish to learn from. Baby fish, it seems, don't know what to eat unless they are taught, and to be taught they need a role model – which can be difficult in captivity, which is where the film came in. The researcher had a lot of nutritious little red worms which wild fish love, but the ones in captivity spurned their meal, so he made a short film showing an adult fish feeding on the small red worms. Before they saw the film the baby fish ignored the worms, but after some showings on a TV placed close to their tank, they were imitating the adult fish in the film – and never went hungry again.

Copying is done by everyone, from the tiniest baby sticking out his tongue when his parents show him how, to adults in a new job mimicking other people's behaviour. It's a wonderful way to learn because it short-circuits experience. By doing what others do and imitating how they behave in different situations, your child will master the most complex skills with precision and pleasure, without having had to work them out from first principles. Gaining expertise is one of the most satisfying things a child can do, and his teachers are

What better proof that children love to copy other people than to see them so exhilarated by success?

numerous; he'll mimic cars on the road, animals, siblings, friends and especially you. He'll learn how you speak, even copy the way you argue. And by the time your baby is one he'll learn to use a trick scientists call 'delayed imitation' – that is, he will visualize what he has seen and re-enact it later.

Once your child can manage delayed imitation he can be creative with everything he sees. He can watch TV and act out the stories; he can watch his friends and do what they do. I remember seeing quite a young child trying to hop across the room and another following suit, which made them both laugh, a moment of joint amusement and communication that excluded everyone else. Perhaps not surprisingly, it turns out that children who spend a lot of time with older children and siblings have an advantage here. Older children are power personified, and offer a big incentive to copy. When a younger child tries to copy an older one he generally gets somewhere – and gets a reaction!

A fascinating fact about our brains

The human brain is designed to make imitation simple – so simple it doesn't need to involve conscious thought. Seeing an action makes certain areas of the brain work and performing the same action a minute later uses exactly the same pathways through the brain. Your child may not even know he is imitating others; only you will recognize that what he is doing is an almost exact reproduction of what he has seen.

And this leads us to an interesting conclusion. Imitation, the pauper of learning skills, all too rarely used as a technique to help children learn from each other at school, may even be an emperor of tools, if only you know how to use it.

BRITT'S STORY

A friend of mine, the sports psychologist Britt Tajet-Foxell, works with the elite of the sporting world. She has helped Olympians win gold medals, Premier League footballers win the Cup and top athletes break world records. Britt told me that the most important attributes of athletes performing at the very top of their game are psychological. Motivation, re-silience, focus and confidence are vital, but there is another thing that can tip the balance: priming the brain by visual-izing the end product, seeing in their mind's eye exactly how they will succeed, is also crucial for a successful outcome. Why is that? Because we can copy something we see in our imagination just as well as something that is real.

A fascinating fact about imitation

An enormous amount of what we think of as 'taking after' our parents is, in fact, the result of careful – albeit unconscious – study and exact copying by our very observant youngsters. Once your child has got these 'ways of doing things' under his belt he'll move on to other things, but the habits he has picked up by watching you will remain fixed, often for ever.

WHAT YOU CAN DO ... for babies

- Babies learn practical skills by mimicry: pushing buttons on the TV, 'reading' a book, splashing soap in the bath and turning on lights.

- All the skills babies learn by imitating go straight into the 'how-to' part of memory. So if you have a meal together, your baby may remember how she uses a spoon but not that you taught her; similarly she will learn to speak by copying, but she'll never know how she did it.

WHAT YOU CAN DO ... for toddlers

- Your child is so confident in his immense capacity to do things, he will reach for the stars – at which point he may need a little help. If a task is beyond him, try breaking it down into its constituent parts and show him how to do each little bit, before joining them back together.
- Children imitate your emotional outbursts – if you laugh a lot, they will do the same and find the same things funny. If you are angry and shout a lot, they will learn that too.
- Children often walk like their parents not because it is genetically inherited, but because they copy you. They also copy phraseology, accents, facial expressions and gestures, which is why adopted children often bear a strong resemblance to their adoptive parents.

- Chatty parents usually produce chatty toddlers, who frequently become articulate adults.
- Children also copy your eating habits. Families who eat together usually like the same food; it is one good way to make sure your child appreciates his vegetables.

WHAT YOU CAN DO ... for older children

- Try listening to families talking together in supermarkets. There's often a lot of shouting and ordering kids about, while others talk to their children and get them to participate. Think how your child's style of communication is modelled on yours. How does he express himself?
- Imitation doesn't have to be all one way – all kids love it if you imitate them, especially if they can pretend to be Mum. And it's funny pretending to be other people as well as a way to develop acting skills.
- And don't forget to encourage your child to use one of the best tools – visualization – which is really imitating doing something, simply by imagining it in your mind.

Exploring

In the exciting world of the explorer, freedom is the law. Disregarding dirt, danger and the despair of loved ones, her sole mission is to unearth the truth.

Your child is an explorer and your job is to feed her huge appetite for knowledge. But can you bring yourself to let her go?

Everyone who has looked after babies and toddlers knows how much they can test your patience, smearing food over their newly washed hair, taking their sibling's favourite things and biting into them, disappearing off only to be found throwing toothbrushes into the toilet. But think again. Is this being bad, or is it being an explorer? From a child's point of view, the world is full of questions begging for answers. What does it feel like to have food in your hair? What's so good about that new toy? Perhaps it tastes delicious. And does Mum's toothbrush sink or swim? What if you flush it?

Children need to be able to experiment and succeed on their own. They are all brave explorers of their small world, naturally inquisitive, testing reality and ready to climb the highest mountain to find things out. No child will learn to walk unless she is willing to fall over. No child will learn to speak unless she is willing to get it wrong. No child will learn to enjoy the world unless she is allowed to explore it.

Thirty years ago, child psychologist Dr Jean Piaget watched his two children closely as they grew up and identified the importance of experimentation in their development. One of his series of observations illustrates this well.

JEAN PIAGET'S STORY

When Jean Piaget's eldest child, Janine, was a very little baby and dropped her toys on the floor, she didn't even look for them, and Piaget reasoned that, to her, they didn't exist; they were, literally, out of mind. Then one day, when she was a few months old, she made a discovery. She looked around and found that the toy she had dropped was on the floor. For months she experimented, dropping everything on to the floor – her cup, her doll and her clothes. In the process she discovered gravity. Her experimenting continued, and by the

time she was one she had discovered something just as important: that things can be found, even if they are out of sight. Piaget tested Janine's discovery by hiding a toy under a cloth, and now, six months older and wiser, she found it.

Would she have learnt the fundamental truths about how objects behave without experimenting? It would certainly have taken longer and not been as much fun.

All children need to learn by trial and error, or rather trial and success. Exploring and experimenting is always successful, because something is always learnt. Each small discovery encourages your child to learn more, until she becomes the complete expert. Many things can only be learnt by exploring.

CHARLIE'S STORY

One day when my son Charlie was very little I watched him doing something he obviously felt was very important. We were in the living room and he was crawling round and round the sofa. He looked underneath it, he pulled himself up to look over it; he pushed the cushions and poked the back rest and rubbed his cheek on the arms. He was really concentrating and didn't want to be deflected. Eventually he looked up at me with a triumphant smile on his face. He had explored every aspect of the sofa and now he seemed to be telling me that he had discovered the essential nature of a sofa, would recognize it again, and he was thoroughly pleased with himself.

A child's hunger for experience is, of course, tempered by a natural wariness of unfamiliar situations, which is why she likes to have someone around to check back with. Watching a one-year-old explore her world is rather like watching someone attached to a long piece of elastic. She will go a certain distance, check you are still there, venture further, get scared and come rushing back to your arms, and then go out again. She will experiment with objects, pushing, throwing, examining and chewing until she has found out everything she can about them, all the while checking back with you. It's the same in all new situations, her powerful instinct to explore competing with her innate caution, and although some children are more adventurous than others, they all have their limits.

While some parents are happy to leave their children to explore to the limits of safety, others find their child's exuberance worrying. Looking at the children I work with, I have noticed that modern life has bred a tendency to over-protect. Instead of letting children find things out for themselves, parents usually tell them what to do. Instead of letting them experiment, they tell them the result, and instead of encouraging them to explore on their own, they tell them

what will happen. Fear is catching; children take on their parents' anxieties and temper their natural exuberance, sometimes to the point where they lose confidence in exploring altogether. Yet children yearn to do things for themselves. For their own self-esteem they need to feel they are an active agent in the world and the excitement a child feels when she makes a discovery is more valuable than any number of scratched knees and bruised elbows she might get along the way.

CARLA'S STORY

Carla was a girl who liked to do things for herself and she was very stubborn. By the time she was six her parents were at their wits' end and truly fed up with trying to persuade her to act against her will. So one day they decided to do an experiment. One of Carla's bugbears was her coat, which she hated, so her mother stopped telling her to wear it, and, for once, Carla was free. She wanted to go out without her coat even though it was a cold day – and she could! But after a few hours she became uncomfortably cold, realized she had made a mistake, and the next day she didn't protest about wearing the coat. Doing what you want is lovely, but (and it is a big but) the difficulty is *knowing* what you want if your parents take too many decisions for you. Experts call this powerful learning tool 'Natural Consequences' because nature itself provides the lessons, and Carla's parents, keen to stop their nagging, decided to use it on a regular basis.

Think how much your child learns by exploring:
- How to love learning by finding things out by herself because she wants to.
- How to make herself confident by proving how clever, persistent and observant she is.
- How to make herself happy by knowing what she wants and how to get it.

WHAT YOU CAN DO ... for all children
- Let her experiment as much as she wants as long as it isn't dangerous.
- Let her play on her own and learn by doing things for herself.
- Keep interruptions to a minimum.
- Let her be imaginative – using saucepans as drums, spoons to make music.
- Let her get dirty.
- Take time to support your child, as she explores her mental and physical limits.
- Appreciate her successes and empathize with any accidents.
- Empower her by letting her learn about natural consequences.

Rote Learning

Do not despise this humble tool! Rote learning gets a bad press as it's supposed to be boring and forced. Quite the contrary. Children love getting things right, which means conscious, intentional learning can be fun. It's under their control and it's the best way to gain some great expertise.

If you think deliberate learning is just something you were forced to do to pass exams, think again. Things you learn with intent – by rote – are things you really want to know, either because you are interested or because knowledge enables understanding. The more you know, the more easily you learn (see Memory Basics, p.123). Rote learning – and being taught – is a quintessentially human activity; no other animal chooses to learn so much apparently irrelevant information. But we do it because we like it.

Children of all ages learn by rote, consciously trying to get things right, but rote learning really comes into its own at the age of three, when you can help your child enjoy learning consciously for its own sake. Your four-year-old child, excited and confident, will seize the opportunity to learn about whatever he is passionate about – football, dinosaurs or cars. And if you support whatever takes his fancy, he will practise what he learns until he can recite it back in his sleep. You have a window of opportunity here to build on your child's enthusiasms and even to imbue a lifelong love of learning.

A fascinating fact about how knowledge has changed

Two years ago we tested the *Child of Our Time* children, then four years old, to find out what they knew about TV. Almost all of them thought that the people were inside the box and that if the TV was turned over, everything would fall out! Looking back, we discovered that twenty years ago kids knew that pictures were transmitted from TV stations; they had been told. TV technology is no longer exciting news and we don't think to talk about it. But I don't think that means we have dumbed down. Children still want to know about rockets and wildlife, and how things work, and because people travel so much, they actually know a good deal more than we used to about different cultures.

Think how many important things children learn by rote:
- Numbers
- Spellings
- Lots of facts
- Nursery rhymes
- Jokes
- Songs.

Parents are usually the best educators of their children. If you want your kids to learn facts and figures, you will teach them, and there are lots of places to go for help. Libraries are not just great places to find new books with your children, from *The Guinness Book of Records* to children's books on history, wildlife or poetry – they also provide activities and storytelling sessions where your child can meet others. Museums can be fascinating too, with interactive exhibitions and quizzes designed specially for kids.

However, the most ubiquitous sources of information and education are now the internet and television. TV is one of the most popular inventions of the modern world; most people wouldn't be without it. And since the amount of time spent viewing has increased rapidly – the average four-year-old watches nearly four hours a day – many parents want to know what, if anything, children gain from it.

There is no doubt that watching programmes specifically designed for children helps them learn new things consciously. Toddlers vary enormously in their enjoyment of television, but most prefer programmes that are made for them, with bright colours, action songs they can join in with, and slow repetitive speech. Under these circumstances they will try hard to learn. Children's programmes are much less didactic than they used to be, nonetheless children learn from them by looking, listening and repeating, just as they always did. But you can't rely on a toddler's undivided attention – most only watch about half of any one programme – so conscious learning tends to be fragmentary and is much more effective if someone is there to help.

MEGAN'S STORY

Gaynor, Rhodri and their children, Dafi-fian, Delana and Megan, live on a farm in Wales. Gaynor credits television with teaching four-year-old Megan to speak English: 'We speak Welsh at home, it's her mother tongue, but Megan learnt English through television and going to nursery where they chant rhymes. She only has to hear them twice now and she's got them by heart. She's learnt the English faster than her brother and sister, because they've explained to her what the words mean on television – they're like little sponges, they just take everything in!'

By the time your child is four his brain will have grown and he will be able to get more out of appropriate programmes, especially ones that include rote learning of letters, numbers and songs. And Children's TV also encourages humour and offers stories strong on the difference between right and wrong – and knowledge about TV characters becomes useful capital in the playground. But research shows that your child will learn much more effectively if he watches television with an adult who can explain what he doesn't understand and answer questions. But there is a health warning! TV can be attractive enough for older children to get stuck in front of it. This problem is even more acute in the case of computer games, which are designed to give constant rewards that can keep children going for hours. There is an obvious reason why that is a problem – children learn much more in the real world.

WHAT YOU CAN DO ... for your toddler and older child

- Your child takes his attitudes from you. If you place a high value on learning, so will he. It is worth being explicit about how important knowledge is and how easy it can be to accrue by following up interests.
- Human beings remember words much more easily if they are put to music, as most of us will realize if we think of all the advertising jingles we know. So singing songs – especially ones you invent

together – is a great way to rote-learn lists and facts. Children of all ages can learn by singing, even if they are out of tune to start with.

- One of the most envied talents is to be able to tell jokes. Jokes almost always have to be learnt by rote, so your child gets a double whammy.
- TV and, especially, computer games need to be carefully monitored and clear time limits imposed. Children need active games to keep their bodies fit and their minds sharp and curious.
- Children love quizzes if they are not too competitive and they can win, hence the eternal popularity of 'I Spy'. You can make up your own, playing on your child's interests and the things around you. You can make up quizzes about anything, from names of relatives and friends for very young children to more complex subjects like names of birds or modes of transport for older ones, and you can make quizzes more fun by adding an element of 'spot the deliberate mistake'.

DO IT YOURSELF: kids' quizzes
- Ask about names – of people, places and countries.
- Ask about groups of objects – like birds or modes of transport.
- Ask about types of activities – like swimming and music.
- Ask about differences –like any difference you can think of between fish and people.
- Ask about similarities – like anything you can think of that is green.
- Ask about opposites – fast/slow, up/down and so on.
- Challenge your child to make sentences where specific words begin with the same letter. For instance: Arthur and Anna were eating Apples on their holiday in Argentina.

  Quizzes have to be tailored to your child's interests and ability, but they can be a lot of fun – especially on car journeys – if done for brief periods of time and if you chat about all the answers rather than just accepting the 'right' one.

If rote learning had really gone out of fashion the symptoms would be obvious – there would be a low level of general knowledge. Tests show that today's children don't know facts their parents or grandparents learnt as a matter of course, but while this generation may not know who is Prime Minister, or the names of capital cities and major world rivers, they do know an enormous number of facts. Historical stories, wildlife, fashion and football are all still on the agenda, and their use of the internet shows how keen they are to find answers to their questions.

As your child enters each new phase of life, one of the most fundamental signs of his development is the way he uses learning to understand and change his world.

He starts life learning by association: the smell of milk means he is about to be fed, and crying summons his carer. He builds on his knowledge, learning by imitation, learning to look where you looked, picking up a spoon to feed himself. Excitement at new-found abilities – turning over, sucking his thumb – encourages him to try more. He starts to experiment, to pull open drawers and kick a football, building on success after success until language comes into play and suddenly he can start to learn by inquiring and listening to the answers – by learning consciously. He can choose to concentrate on dinosaurs or dolls or anything else that takes his fancy, and he will practise what he has learnt until he can recite it back or do it in his sleep.

Unconsciously, but with great perspicacity, your child has discovered that he can use all the learning techniques in combination. Complex tasks require different combinations, but there are some principles that will help your child target his efforts and get results.

How to use basic principles to teach your child to learn a complex activity. For instance, kicking a football into a net.

- Start by showing him the whole process: kicking a ball into the net.
- Next break it down into small steps: where on the ball he should kick, which side of the foot to use and where to look, etc.
- Let him experiment with the task, and refine his movements.
- Show him how to use his body and ask him to imitate you.
- Let him ask questions and find his own answers.
- Then extend him: as he gains accuracy, move the net gradually away.
- Show him the whole movement again slowly, but using all your power.
- Then show him the best: watch a professional footballer on TV or go to see a match.
- Ask him to visualize the movement and practise in his mind again and again.
- And then try again – he will succeed beyond your wildest dreams!

These principles can be used to teach pretty much anything and the more your child learns, the more techniques he will develop to get him on his way. This is how intelligence is built.

PART TWO

GET MOTIVATED!

Motivation is the spur that creates effort. Without motivation, our brains would have atrophied, there would be no inventions and no civilization. Motivation generates happiness, and the exultation we gain from learning new things.

KEITH AND FRANCESCA'S STORY

On a cold, rainy January day, Keith and Francesca were born into families who lived on opposite sides of the road in an unremarkable British town. Their parents were neither rich nor poor; just ordinary people who worried about ordinary problems: money, jobs and children. Keith was an outgoing little boy and, as his early tests showed, very clever. Francesca was a skinny child, more anxious and clearly less bright, but kind and obedient.

As expected, Keith learnt rapidly when he started school, while Francesca plodded along behind. But over the years their positions gradually reversed, and by the end of their seventh year, Francesca had begun to shine. Her Maths and English scores were impressive and she looked set for a glittering school career. Keith, however, was in trouble. He had fallen behind; his scores were now only just average, and dropping away year on year.

Eleven years later found Francesca at a top university, and four years after that she became a journalist; a rising star on a major national newspaper. So what had happened to Keith? Disillusioned by school failure, he had left at sixteen to work behind a bar, and at twenty-two was still looking for a career.

Looking back, this trajectory was almost inevitable. Stubborn, obedient Francesca stuck at her tasks and as she learnt facts she absorbed a work ethic that drove her on. Her parents, uncertain of her likely achievements, were careful to help her focus and boosted her self-belief. But Keith always thought he was owed success. His parents had lower expectations and their constant admiration acted as a brake on his ambition. He felt no need to stretch himself and gradually he lost his way.

All of us can lose motivation for specific tasks, but why should a talented young child become so catastrophically unmotivated that his education is brought to a halt? And what can parents do to make sure their child gets through the bad times with the will to achieve still intact?

Shakespeare's definition of motivation is still in today's dictionaries. Motivation, he said, is 'the whole of that which moves, excites or invites the Mind to Volition'. That is, motivation is what makes us take action. So what sorts of things motivate us? And why?

Over the years I have explored much scientific and psychological literature to find out why some of us are motivated to take positive action in the world and some of us just aren't. In the next six chapters I will show you what you can do to improve your child's sense of agency through the various factors that create and sustain motivation. They are positivity, self-belief, concentration, resilience, hard work and rewards. But first, some motivational basics.

Motivational Basics

Motivation is one of the most important gifts you can give your child. A child who willingly engages with whatever activity comes her way is on the way to becoming a happy, successful adult.

Everyone – even the laziest person in the world – is motivated by some of the following ten imperatives.

1 Force of nature: we are impelled to do some things – eat, sleep, keep ourselves and our children warm and safe.
2 Buying into a collective identity: obeying rules and doing jobs because we will be blamed if we don't is a big part of most of our lives.
3 Making life better: we want to reach our goal get a qualification, go for promotion, learn to drive or retire from work.
4 Giving pleasure: we feel good when we please someone – take a friend out, buy a present, give to charity.
5 Concentrating on something: we feel exhilarated because we have been totally immersed in doing a difficult puzzle, some DIY or reading a book.
6 Being inventive: we feel good because we have created some thing new – painted a picture, invented a new recipe or improved a garden.
7 Achieving something: we feel good because we have done something admirable – scoring a tricky goal in a football match or hosting a wonderful party.
8 Being part of a group: we want to make friends, work harmoniously with others, look after a family.
9 Winning: we like to feel better than others – more important and more powerful, able to be successful in life's competitions.
10 Sheer enjoyment: we want to feel happy – whether having fun with friends, climbing a mountain or curling up in front of the television.

In spite of the need to do, we often don't. Instead we let 'I can't' overtake us and opportunities are lost. Think of how many times you have let things fall out of your grasp just because you can't bring yourself to get over a psychological barrier – fear, laziness, feeling doomed to failure, lacking real intent, or not knowing what you actually want. Our impulses to remain inert often have their source in childhood.

We may be determined to do what we know would be valuable, but there are opposing forces that can stop us doing things – forces that are demotivating, especially for children.

1 Boredom: dull repetitive work demotivates everyone. The only thing that can make it bearable is a reward, a sense of duty – or daydreams.
2 Lack of self-worth: feeling unloved and unappreciated makes children lose faith in themselves and become self-critical and negative.
3 Fear of failure: many children are not resilient enough. Criticism, ridicule or accidents can stop them in their tracks.
4 Sense of helplessness: constant failure over a period of time can lead to the belief that we will always fail, and that stops us trying.
5 Low expectations: if nothing is expected it's hard to make any effort, so nothing is achieved.
6 Lack of responsibility: children find it easy to pass the buck to their parents, but this is counterproductive. Motivation has to come from a personal desire for activity.
7 Lack of concentration. Some people are easily distracted and find it hard to enjoy any activity for very long, so motivation can be hard to sustain.
8 Lack of control. Demands that cannot be met are very demotivating, whether they are because of a skills discrepancy or external factors like poverty, too much pressure or bullying siblings.
9 Can't be bothered. This is usually in response to an activity that your child feels is not worth doing or the reaction to an activity that someone else wants her to do and she doesn't.
10 Lack of energy. Clearly fatigue, depression, stress or illness can make it extremely difficult to rise to a challenge.

Being fearful, bored or demotivated is a depressing way for any child to live, while being motivated, more often than not, imbues us with energy and makes us feel good. So what can we do to help? There

are various ways that children can be encouraged to feel motivated, through the right use of rewards and the development of self-belief, resilience and concentration, but they are all dependent on one simple tool …

'I am the Greatest!' Mohammed Ali knew that the right words at the right time are the greatest motivator of all. Words can make us want to rise up and do something. You can make your child feel that whatever she is doing is exciting and important just by the power of your talk. You can make her feel heroic, loved and special.

How To Talk So Children Will Listen

The way you talk to your child can change her life. Here are five tips on talking:

1 To motivate your child, make eye contact, get to your child's level, state your message clearly, keep sentences short and tailored to her age, add in your feelings and let her ask questions. Children listen when they are certain you are focused and when you are talking about things they can see, hear or feel.
2 Scaffold motivation (see p.68) by offering ideas to help her extend herself into zones just outside her current capabilities and exuding confidence in her ability to do it.
3 Use praise and blame judiciously, praising effort rather than achievement and acknowledging specific details rather than making blanket statements (see p.76 for how to praise).

4 If your child is feeling down, cheer her up by following up her wishes with fantasies: 'I wish we could go out too – what is the most exciting journey we could take?'

5 And if your child is cross, share your values – 'I can see you are angry, but it isn't right to hit' – and then boost her morale – 'So what could you have done differently?'

… And here are five tips on how not to talk!

1 If you lecture or give too many unexplained orders your child will feel helpless and resentful.

2 If you force advice – 'Do this and it will be OK' – you stop her thinking and reduce her confidence. Instead, try offering help – 'How would you feel about …?', 'Would you consider …?'

3 If there is a problem, try not to respond angrily as she will feel blamed rather than won over. Instead give her choices: 'If you help now, I will help you later.' Or use neutral statements: 'The damp towel is making the floor wet.' She will probably pick it up!

4 If you discount her feelings with 'No need to cry' or 'You'll soon feel better', she is less likely to confide in you.

5 If you make yourself unavailable too often, and communicate important messages while doing something else, she will feel as if you don't care.

How To Listen So Children Will Talk

The way you listen to your child can also change her world. Here are five tips on how to listen:

1 Consider your child's ideas with respect, assuming that she means well and is competent and responsible.

2 Be patient, she may need to do some ciphering to put her ideas into words.

3 Use reflective listening, repeating back what she has said and asking her if you have got it right. She will feel understood and encouraged to tell you more.

4 If she asks a question, ask her what she thinks before you give your answer. It helps her think, makes her feel clever, and gives you a glimpse into her world.

5 If she knows you are really listening with your whole being she will tell you her secrets.

… And five tips on how not to listen!

1 If you ignore your child's feelings and just tell her what to do, she will clam up. Instead, acknowledge them with a short agreement or 'hmm' and she'll probably tell you more.

2 If you jump to conclusions and don't use reflective listening she is more likely to think you don't listen at all.

3 If you blame her she'll be angry. Instead, listen hard and encourage her to tell you the details. That way you'll get the whole story.

4 If she has a problem that's bugging you, don't think you necessarily have the solution. Instead, listen to her ideas, as she's likely to be able to put them into practice.

5 If your child is burning to talk, try not to put her off; she lives in the moment so you may never have a second chance.

Talking and listening openly with your child is always important and it is profoundly influenced by your own unconscious style, as 'A Day in the Lab' with mums and dads proved …

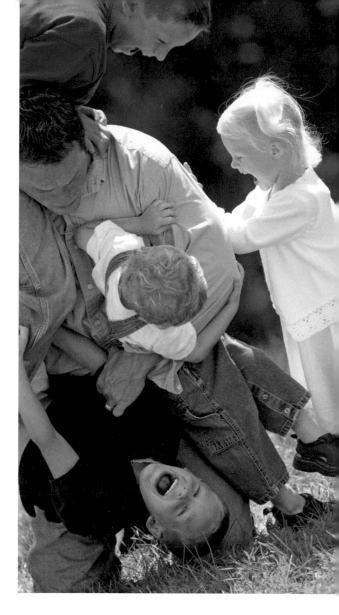

A DAY IN THE LAB

Years ago I noticed that mums and dads tend to communicate differently with their children. Dads are often rougher and more physical, mums more chatty and more artistic. So how do parents compare when they play the same game? The *Child of Our Time* team decided to find out by giving parents a line drawing of a house, and a drawing toy called 'Etch-a-sketch' with two knobs, one marking vertical lines, the other horizontal lines, and instructing them to work with their four-year-old to copy the sketch. The results were polarized. The mothers were generally hands-off and talked about the task, encouraging their child to do the best they could. The drawings, on the whole, were terrible, but the children had done the work themselves. The fathers were more dictatorial, they tended to take more control of the knobs, issuing a stream of precise instructions. Unsurprisingly the pictures they made, with the children helping, were much more accurate.

During this game the children received two different, but equally important, lessons in motivation. Their mothers' positive chat gave them the chance to practise and make mistakes without criticism, whereas learning with their more competitive fathers proved that, with intensive verbal training, this difficult task was within their mutual grasp, and that it is also important to succeed by other people's standards.

WHAT YOU CAN DO ... for all children

- Listen and talk to your child (see tips above).
- Use 'scaffolding' (see below) to encourage your child to learn.
- Make sure your child knows how much you enjoy her company.
- Keep your specific suggestions simple and think about whether you communicate at a level she understands.
- Encourage her to take the lead in whatever task she is doing, and also promote the idea that she should aim high.
- Don't insist on her doing anything. Instead let her stop when she wants to. She will lose motivation if she feels pushed, or is bored, cold, hungry or tired.
- You are a powerful role model. So demonstrate your own high level of motivation and tell her about the things you enjoy.

WHAT YOU CAN DO ... for your baby

- If you want to motivate your baby there is a wonderful technique you can use, called 'scaffolding'. It works for all children and will be mentioned many times in this book. The guiding principle is to help your baby to learn slowly and incrementally, building on each achievement, and to do that you have to work with what she can almost do. If your child is waving her hand at a toy that is just out of swiping range, move the toy in slightly and she'll succeed in touching it. That will encourage her to have another go. If she is trying to look at a squashy toy but can't keep her head in the right position, move the toy (or her head) so she can see it. Next time, she'll know better which way to turn. Scaffolding helps a child grow in dexterity and understanding, where each small achievement is a vital step forward, and it is a brilliant and simple motivational tool.

JOLY'S STORY

I was in a coffee bar a few weeks ago and witnessed a perfect example of scaffolding. A young woman had met with three friends and was engaged in a lively discussion. Her baby, called Joly, sat on his mother's lap but was otherwise, it seemed, completely ignored. There was an intriguing shiny spoon close by, which he picked up and immediately dropped on the floor. Without thinking, his mother passed it back with a grin and a kiss. The conversation continued, the baby swiped the spoon, and it flew out of reach. One of the friends pushed it back with an encouraging word, and Joly stretched to reach it and banged the table with it. The long coffee break became lunch, the talk never stopped, but all the time Joly was getting just enough sensitive, finely tuned help from the adults to enable him to do something that was slightly beyond his capabilities. Gradually I saw him mastering handling the spoon because he wanted to learn and wasn't left to fail. Whatever he wanted to try, he could, and it was never so difficult that he became discouraged and fractious.

WHAT YOU CAN DO ... for your toddler

- By the time your baby has become a toddler she will want to be more in control of her learning. Most toddlers are hugely motivated; this is an age when letting her have fun and take the lead is important, but she also needs to feel safe with you close at hand. Scaffolding principles apply for toddlers too – so support her small steps, extend her knowledge and keep it light-hearted.
- Humans always want to know why. If you explain why you want your child to do something, she is much more likely to give it a go. She'll put the information away for next time – and probably repeat it back!
- Having a laugh while learning is enormously motivating, as the following interchange, where Gillian sensitively supports her son William's learning, shows:

Gillian and William speak

William:	(*aged two*): The spider, the spider.
Gillian:	(*aged thirty-two*):
	The spider on the tractor. What's a spider doing on a tractor?
William:	There's a bee in there.
Gillian:	You don't like bees, do you?

William:	Because the – it hurt my finger.
Gillian:	Do you like dinosaurs?
William:	No. I don't like T-Rex. He runs very fast.
Gillian:	He moves very fast. Do you think that if he caught you he'd gobble you up?
William:	I don't know. T-Rex is going away and the butterfly going away.
Gillian:	Only the butterfly can fly, yes.
William:	T-Rex he say Rrrrrrrrrrrrrrr.
Gillian:	You know what T-Rex does. And what do butterflies do?
William:	Oh, butterfly can't say Rrrrrrrrrrrrrrr, he go flutter, flutter, flutter.
Gillian:	Flutter, flutter, flutter – aah. What do cows say?
William:	Mooooooooooooooo.
Gillian:	And what do sheep say?
William:	(*laughing*): BANG! BANG! BANG!

WHAT YOU CAN DO ... for your older child

- You can increase her motivation by telling her what you expect of her in general terms: to work hard, to enjoy challenges, and to pursue her interests, as she is likely to internalize those messages. But she will get the message even more clearly if you spend plenty of time introducing her to a new activity – she will realize straight away that this one is important to you!

- Your child will know exactly what she wants and will ask lots of questions. Answer them! You don't need to bore her with long explanations or too many facts; short answers and encouragement are all she needs.

- As children grow they become more certain about what they like, and, crucially, what they dislike. They are often impatient, especially of other people's needs. But older children also want to learn and keeping them motivated does not need to be hard if you play into their passions and can joke about your differences.

PATTY'S STORY

Many parents like to take their children to a museum for its educational value and because it can play to the family's diverse interests. But, as I have found over the years, visiting a museum with small children can easily become a nightmare. A few months ago my friend Alice recounted her heart-sink moment – and how she got out of it.

Alice's trip had been organized by her feisty six-year-old, Patty, who had heard from a friend that the local transport museum was fantastic. Her little brother, four-year-old Gram, was not keen but agreed to go because of the tractors, so Alice took them both one Saturday afternoon. Patty walked through the door with high hopes, took one look at all the motionless vehicles and immediately declared it was boring. Disappointment made her angry and she wanted to go straight home. Gram had the opposite response to the museum; but he was also angry because Patty was spoiling everything. Not an auspicious start, but Alice is a trained teacher and knew what to do. She took them both to the museum café and used the time to listen to what they didn't like and point out some things she thought they would enjoy. The museum itself was still a no-go area for Patty but there were funny chocolate tractors in the shop and a visitor with a guide dog. Patty loved dogs. By the time the afternoon was over Patty had been all round the museum with the dog-owner, carefully explaining the exhibits to the dog and making sure he didn't get into the cars and trains, and Gram had raced up and down the platforms and in and out of all the vehicles, dragging Alice down to coal bunkers and up to the top of double-decker buses. And the whole family had learnt something: there are many ways to be motivated; it's just a matter of finding the right line of attack.

Nowadays many parents believe that it is best to give children as much choice as they can, but motivating independent minds that question authority is a much more complex proposition than insisting on blind obedience, even though it pays dividends because children who learn how to motivate themselves early are likely to be proactive for the rest of their lives.

I have done a lot of research to find out precisely what parents can do to promote motivation in children. Rewards and punishments are widely and successfully used as strategies to encourage children to achieve and there are also three important personal characteristics – self-belief, resilience and concentration – that need to be built. The next four chapters explore these, starting with meting out rewards and punishments, which is one of the trickiest strategies to get right.

How to Use Rewards

There is one force of nature you can take advantage of and that is the universal desire of children to be the apple of their parents' eye. Children love parental attention, more than virtually anything else. Attention is a reward more potent than strawberries and ice-cream, but, if it's to work, it must be used wisely.

PROFESSOR B. F. SKINNER'S STORY

In 1931 the influential American psychologist Professor Burrhus Skinner embarked on a series of experiments that was to make him famous. He wanted to understand the forces that motivate us and, when he was only a student, built a learning box for rats, known ever since as the 'Skinner Box'. Rats are friendly and intelligent animals and Skinner knew they would be curious enough to find that pressing a lever released a reward – in this case, food. And he was right, the rats quickly learnt the box's secrets. Then, over a period of years, Skinner uncovered the laws of rewards: how and why we behave and what sorts of rewards work best. In particular, he found that rats trained to expect a reward every time they pressed the lever stopped pressing as soon as the reward stopped appearing. But if he started them on a stop-go regime with the reward sometimes available and sometimes not, the rats never stopped looking for it. Skinner reasoned that intermittent rewards were the most powerful of all, for humans as well as animals. Why? Because you set up the hope of a reward with the knowledge that it might not be there, so there is no reason ever to give up.

Skinner's ideas revolutionized psychology because his principles of learning are not only correct, they actually work.

The truth is that human beings are motivated by rewards just as much as any other species, but have complex, and sometimes contradictory, needs. Different types of reward compete for predominance: physical needs like the need for food vie with the desire for status and power, or the pleasure that comes with giving competes with the

What the New Ford Will Do
PAGE 134

Ads before (below right) and after the J.B. Watson revolution

urge to win. Being active is another vital source of well-being – to be is to do. And, of course, there are material goods, from sweets to gifts. So increasing your child's motivation requires a balance, where all motivating forces with their attendant rewards are fostered in the restraining context of social pressure and moral values.

A fascinating fact about using rewards to fuel the market

Humans are motivated by a complex set of desires, but none is more important to the human psyche than the need for status, as psychologist Professor John Watson realized in the late 1920s when he changed from academic psychologist to wealthy father of modern advertising, transforming the humble information-giving advertisement into a sales pitch that imbued a product with glamour and status. This was exceedingly successful for good reason. By its very nature, the product that offers a glamorous lifestyle rarely grants the buyer the promised happiness for long. So it was that Watson hooked customers into the treadmill of consumerism by offering intermittent rewards. Just like Professor Skinner's rats, the human consumer is motivated to go for the reward again, and again.

How Many Buyers Can Judge *Value?*

NEARLY every man has his visions of finding the ideal motor car. He anticipates the true mastery of the roads at last, and the prestige of being *right* at every point of his motoring.

For the man who wants the Packard qualities in his motoring, only the Packard Car will do. While if his taste and sense of values are not up to the Packard, some other car will do.

The Packard Twin-Six really is as true and fine as anyone ever assumed any car to be.

It occupies, alone and sufficient, the place it has made for itself. It stands aloof equally from the car that obviously can be no better than it looks, and from the car that

strives to look better than it is.

The dominant place of the Packard is not a thing of chance. For twenty-one years the Packard has been delivering *intrinsic value—* the soundest value a motor car has ever given.

During the War, inspecting officers spoke of the Packard plant as a manufacturing marvel. The only automobile plant in the world to produce high-grade cars on a quantity basis.

Why this tremendous plant investment? Simply to produce a car of Packard grade at a price within reason. If built by piecemeal methods the Packard would be the highest priced car in the world.

PACKARD MOTOR CAR COMPANY · DETROIT

Children who have internalized ambitions – who are motivated to learn because they like it – are the lucky ones. They don't need pushing or punishing, they just get on with it. We all want children like that and all children can be like that, if we use rewards wisely. But a simple experiment we did with a bunch of school children shows how easy it is to get it wrong, even with a simple reward such as an inexpensive toy.

A DAY IN THE LAB: a cautionary tale about rewards

We did a fascinating experiment that showed, in just half an hour, that motivation is easy if you do it right! We started by asking a class of five-year-olds to tell us if they liked drawing. A forest of waving hands showed that they did. Then we divided the children into three groups. The first group was asked to draw a picture for fun; they got no reward. The second group was asked to draw a picture and was given a surprise reward after they had finished. The last group was told they would get a reward – a little toy – if they drew a picture. Then we settled back to watch what would happen. The first thing we noticed was that all the children got on with their pictures with enthusiasm – they really *did* like drawing! At the end of five minutes we asked them to give us their pictures and gave the promised reward to the third group, the unexpected reward to the second and nothing to the first, and then we left them alone. What happened next was startling. The children in Group Three, who had been told they would get a reward for their drawing, put down their pens and paper – they wanted to do anything but draw. Those in Group Two who had received an unexpected reward started to draw with renewed enthusiasm, and the children in Group One, who had had no reward, also settled happily back to drawing.

So what generated such impressive enthusiasm in the first two groups and what had gone wrong for the rewarded children? For our unrewarded group the answer is clear. They liked drawing and there was no reason to stop. But why had receiving a reward stifled, rather than fuelled, Group Three's ambition? The reward had changed their attitude. Now they weren't drawing for fun, they were working for a bribe, and they were not going to perform without one.

So what about Group Two, the children whose reward was unexpected? The good news is that they would have gone on drawing for longer even than our unrewarded group. To a parent that might seem like a good outcome. But is it? The trouble is that dangling rewards changes our children's point of view. Instead of drawing because they like it, they are hoping for another reward. The quality of their work decreases because, much like Skinner's rats or gambling adults, they don't care what they do, but are propelled to go on just in case they hit the jackpot.

This experiment shows precisely why bribes don't work. They are fine as a short-term measure to avert revolt when you need your child to be compliant and he's digging his heels in, but in the long term, internalized rewards like genuine pleasure and feeling appreciated work much better.

Appreciation is, in fact, very potent and a lot of people believe that praising their children every time they do anything is the right thing to do. They are right in one way – children *do* need to be praised, just like the rest of us. But, like more tangible rewards such as toys or money, appreciation, too, should be used cautiously. So what should you do?

How to Praise Your Child

Children have complex responses to praise. Here are three different scenarios:

ONE Your child is building a castle from bricks. He finishes it and you say, 'Well done, aren't you a clever boy?'

TWO Your child is building a castle from bricks. While he is doing it you say, 'That looks interesting. I notice you have made the wall yellow and green. I like that.'

THREE Your child is building a castle from bricks. He finishes it. You say nothing and he knocks it down straight away. You say, 'That's a shame. I wanted to see it properly– it looked good.'

Which one do you do the most of? Why?

ONE

This is what most people tend to do. It is nice to be praised and your child will feel proud of himself because you have appreciated his achievements. But your praise is not necessarily motivating, for three reasons:

a He may see it as an indiscriminate reward given by you every time he does anything, and therefore worthless, since he doesn't need to work hard to get it.

b He may like the reward but find it demotivating, finding he is doing the activity for praise and losing his internal motivation – enjoyment.

c Or you may be the sort of parent who only praises success, in which case he may believe that you wouldn't like it if he didn't finish or if it had gone wrong.

This last point is the most interesting, because your child is a great strategist. If he thinks you like him to succeed or dislike failure he is likely either to go for a very easy option or to attempt a difficult one. The easy option arises if you are not very discriminating with your praise. The ultimate strategist, your child will quickly realize that doing an easy task well will get him all the praise he needs. It's the lazy route to success! The more demanding parent, however, only praises results if they are difficult to achieve. Being competitive, wanting your praise and being aware of your high expectations will spur your child to try hard. This can be a good thing; the downside comes if he feels he must be perfect to be worthy of praise. His strategy is then to drive himself too hard. Children in this situation may be very successful but neurotic!

TWO

This is the most effective form of praise, especially if it is given intermittently. You are showing your appreciation of his efforts, whether he succeeds or not. Children who are praised like this are likely to become more creative and happily successful, confident that their mistakes are less important than their efforts. Notice also that the praise in this case is not for the whole task but for a particular element. It shows him that you have noticed not just that he is doing something, but what he is doing. (Tempting as it is, don't make suggestions unless he asks; they may seem interfering and critical.) Appreciation like this breeds resilience and concentration; he is motivated by his own internal goals and when he fails it is on his terms, not yours. He is most likely to blame any poor performance on lack of effort rather than lack of ability.

THREE

The last reaction may have been meant as praise, but could be felt as criticism. He obviously didn't want to keep the castle – perhaps because he wanted to see the crash or the game was finished or it wasn't right. Possibly he would have liked you to comment appreciatively earlier, but you missed the chance.

Praising effort rather than ability is a good habit to get into, because you are really praising motivation, giving him the confidence to try and the courage to fail. And there is a lesson here for parents, too. If you have tendencies to perfectionism or defeatism, you may use those standards to judge your own child-rearing, to your and your children's cost. Bringing up children is not a question of success or failure; as with so much else, it is the effort that counts.

The obverse to rewards is punishment. Most children understand that punishment is sometimes due and are quite resilient; they know that when they have done wrong, they will be told off, or given some more formal warning, like being put in the 'naughty' corner. In the context of an accepted practice, punishment can be part of a repertoire of actions that motivate children to achieve in a social and moral world. But watch out! Children can also experience punishment in surprising ways. Have you ever felt that your child is doing something naughty on purpose? Most of us have. Some children are frequently naughty just to make you cross and it doesn't take long to work out why. Being naughty gains them more attention than being good! It's usually best to ignore bad behaviour as much as possible, and give attention when all is well.

Unfair punishments, however, are extremely demotivating. If a child feels unfairly treated – for instance, told off for something his brother did or given a bad mark at school when he tried his best – he will reject the accusation and, possibly, the person who made it. When a child loses faith in an adult, their ability to motivate him is undermined and regaining trust can take some time.

Another demotivating factor can be adults who snipe, unfairly criticize or nag. Slowly a child will absorb their negative view, and start to become the person the adult seems to have expected – a negative, unenthusiastic person whose self-belief is corroded and whose expectations are low. The reverse, of course, also happens. If you are lucky enough to have a child who admires you, that admiration will help to increase his belief in himself and widen his ambitions.

DO IT YOURSELF : Your praise *v.* punishment audit

Most parents make negative comments about their child's actions many times a day, usually much more often than they praise him.

Listen to yourself for half a day spent with your child and write down the tally to find out how often your child hears you praise or speak appreciatively to him and how often you chastise or speak negatively. The question is: do you catch him being good as often, more often or less often, than you catch him being bad?

I have worked with parents who demonstrate a wide range of styles, from catching their children being bad over seventy-five times in a day and never praising, to parents who catch their children being good more often than not (though in my experience the latter is really rather rare). So where do you stand on the praise–criticism curve?

In fact, experts recommend that children should be appreciated five times as often as they are chastised.

Violence, be it physical or verbal, is always unfair, in that the perpetrator has all the power so it will feel humiliating, intrusive and subjugating. A child exposed regularly to aggression may end up in a state of frustrated compliance, roughly where his parent wants him. But underneath he will be resentful and probably self-hating, believing that he deserves to be hit. Other methods, like avoiding a difficult situation or physically removing a child from it, talking sharply or diverting him, work better in the long term. (The effects of punishment and how to help a discouraged child are discussed further in Chapter Twelve.)

WHAT YOU CAN DO ... for all children

- Remember that attention is rewarding, so notice when he is good and try to ignore bad behaviour. If you can't ignore it, keep your temper and quietly stop him with the minimum of attention.
- It's more motivating to praise for effort than for ability, and praising or criticizing your child's *actions* is much more effective than praising or talking unkindly about your child's *personality* because if you do this he won't remember what you thought about his actions, only that you like or dislike him.

WHAT YOU CAN DO ... for babies

- Babies understand a great deal, so you can do everything in the list above, adjusted to his age. When he's contented, reflect back positive feelings so he sees you are pleased, praise him for effort and be gentle but firm when he takes something he shouldn't.
- But babies are different in one way – they are never bad! They cry because they need you, not because they are being naughty, and you need to pay attention because it is only when your baby feels safe and happy that he will be motivated to learn.

WHAT YOU CAN DO ... for toddlers

- Be specific and give reasons when you praise him – 'I liked it when you did that because ...' and when you are cross – 'I feel angry because ...'
- Think about your child's personality: people are complex, motivated for different reasons, so help him to do things he wants to do as well as the things you want him to do!
- Praise him for effort when he has really tried, even if you may be disappointed in the results, and do so by describing what you really think is good – 'You spent a lot of time putting lovely green spots in this picture' – and make sure it's true! Your child will smell a lie.

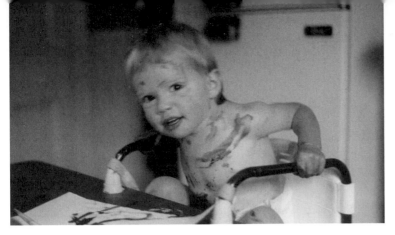

WHAT YOU CAN DO ... for older children

- If you need to help your child, it is much more effective to give him positive messages, to help him visualize the positive rather than the negative, which will increase the chances of the outcome being positive too. For instance, if he is in danger of spilling his drink, ask him to keep the water in the cup, rather than telling him not to drip water on the floor, because visualizing something makes it more likely to happen.

- If an accident has already happened, try not to get angry. First appreciate what he is trying to do: 'I know you like donkeys and want to make a lovely picture,' then make eye contact and explain your problem: 'but I am not happy that you've spattered brown paint all over the floor', and ask him to address the problem: 'so can you help me by clearing it up?' If he doesn't want to, repeat your request until he agrees, then say 'thank you' and 'you did a good job there!' and let that be the end of it.

A fascinating fact about thinking

Try this:

Think of a green elephant.
Now think of a blue elephant
But don't think of a green elephant
What are you thinking of now?!

You, like everyone else, will be thinking of the green elephant because we are are all superb visualizers. Give us a vivid description and we imagine it, and if we imagine something we are just that bit closer to doing it.

How to Foster Self-Belief

'Whether you think you can or think you can't, you're probably right.' Industrialist Henry Ford knew a thing or two about people. Self-belief is absolutely fundamental to successful learning. With it you can fly high; without it, you'll always feel that you could have done better.

Self-belief is about thinking you can succeed. Not everyone has that confidence, even for something quite simple ...

A DAY IN THE LAB

Trying to get a couple of adults to learn one new task provided the *Child of Our Time* team with a great deal of amusement ...

Andy:	Right, here we go, set the date and time on the video.
Researcher:	Setting the timer on a video recorder isn't particularly difficult.
Andy:	I have absolutely no idea how to do it.
Beryl:	I can't, I'm sorry, I've never done it. I've never done it and it's no good!
Researcher:	There's always the instruction manual.
Andy:	I don't do instructions.
Beryl:	My husband always does it.
Researcher:	You're not really trying.
Beryl:	I'm just useless! Absolutely useless!
Andy:	I don't care whether it's set or not, I really just don't care.
Beryl:	I've failed the experiment!

Even for people with high self-esteem, there are always some tasks that defeat them, but they can shrug off failure because they believe in themselves. They tend to be happy, are often extrovert and feel in control most of the time. Most are comfortable with the way they are, which means that they don't feel as if they are failing in life, even when they are failing in a particular task. People with high self-esteem judge themselves more leniently, think they are more intelligent and fun, and tend to be healthier than those with low self-esteem.

A fascinating fact about gender and self-esteem

Contrary to popular belief, women tend to have higher self-esteem and gain in confidence as they get older, unlike men, who seem to lose confidence as they get older. The genders are at their strongest in different domains. Women are happier with their family, more cheerful about their lives and, perhaps surprisingly, happier about their looks. But men's great strength lies where women are weakest – in sport and physical activity, where they score twice as highly as the women.

None of us is confident about everything and your child's self-belief, like that of the adults around her, is likely to be situation specific: for instance, she may be confident socially but cautious physically. The same is true of learning: some children are confident about learning new facts and skills, others are not.

KIM'S STORY

Kim was a chirpy seven-year-old, the third child of two professors who taught at a prestigious university. Happy in her social world, Kim didn't want to learn. She rejected books, hated maths and was disdainful of her older sisters' achievements at school. Kim wanted to leave school as soon as possible and train as a make-up artist.

Kim's dislike of learning had its roots in her early life. Her mother, Angela, had lost a baby boy, and when Kim was born this death profoundly affected their relationship. Angela found it hard to bond with her new baby and Kim started life feeling unwanted. Angela, however, was not neglectful, and fell back on something she knew all about – education. By the time Kim was three she had a huge vocabulary and was beginning to learn to read, albeit slowly. But Kim wasn't, it seemed, as enthusiastic as her sisters and she preferred physical exercise over anything cerebral. Angela found this predilection rather annoying and was slightly offended. Neither of her other children had resisted her help. She started to be critical, blaming Kim for her lack of interest rather than realizing that reading didn't satisfy this daughter's needs. She compared her unfavourably with her sisters and sighed a lot. Kim started to feel incapable and stupid, and fell back on buffoonery to rescue her tattered self-belief. Reading became a no-go area, its aura of failure affecting mother and child.

Kim took these beliefs about herself to school, and, though much loved by staff and children, landed up in the 'time-out' area more than once. An encouraging teacher got her reading, but it wasn't a happy process and Kim would stalk off angrily when she felt forced. Yet Kim was an intelligent child, so what was the real problem?

Academic ability is a very specific area of expertise and Kim's belief that she didn't have it had taken root in her subconscious so early it had become a significant part of her identity. Her angry response to anyone who proved her wrong was the result of feeling her character was under attack. And the fear of failure that hovered in her mind felt so normal she couldn't even name it.

Low self-esteem is not that uncommon in children, but a sense of failure can be conquered with the right encouragement and absolute confidence in your child's abilities.

Children of any age can feel unappreciated. A baby trying to feed herself may be told she is too messy, a toddler building a tower may be told she is clumsy when it falls, and a three-year-old, trying to read, may be laughed at. For some children, failure is everywhere. But if parents decide to abandon the notion of failure altogether, children don't need to be crushed. An experiment that goes wrong is still a success, because it gives you good information about how to do things better! The Nobel Prize-winning scientist Peter Medawar pointed out that his inspired breakthrough was simply due to 'treasuring his failures', and if you and your children treasure failures, rather than be depressed by them, learning will happen faster and more happily.

A DAY IN THE LAB

The American psychologist Martin Seligman wanted to solve a conundrum. Was it genes or environment that made some people unable to do much with their lives, while others believe that everything they do will work out well? How, he wondered, do we become optimists or pessimists? The same personality traits can also occur in animals, as Seligman knew from studying dogs. He trained them to be frightened of an electric fence and then put them in a pen where the fence was not switched on. A dog who had been frequently

frightened by the electric fence in the first place never even tried to get out of the second pen, even though the fence wasn't switched on. That dog had turned his face to the wall and was seriously demotivated. Martin Seligman called this 'learned helplessness'. Humans can develop learned helplessness too, and, while there may be some genetic predisposition to depression, learned helplessness is very largely caused by feeling impotent and a failure far too often. Some of us end up feeling this way permanently, and most of us experience some moments when expectations of failure haunt us and, like Martin Seligman's dogs, we just can't be bothered to go on.

Learned helplessness is not uncommon, and some of its symptoms will be familiar to almost everyone. So why do so many of us get into this sorry state?

Olivia speaks

Olivia has suffered from a sense of failure for many years and tends to shy away from anything challenging. She has learned helplessness, but why?

> " I was bullied and picked on at school. If I needed to go to the toilet I'd pack up my things because I thought when I came back everything would be missing, or someone would have spat in my bag.
> I thought I was probably the worst person in the class and I wouldn't put my hand up and ask for help because I was worried that people would laugh. And before I'd even attempt a piece of work I'd look at it and just go, 'Oh I can't do that, I'm stupid.' I loved Art, and I'd really like to go back and re-do my exams but I feel if I was in a class situation again I'd be the only one in there that was struggling, I'd still be the stupid one. I feel I'm rubbish at everything and now I worry that I'm failing my children. I get the fear back as soon as I look at their homework. Even when I know I've got their sums or spelling right I feel frightened. "

Learned helplessness is built through the constant interplay between what a child does and the reception she gets from others – especially, when she is young, from her parents. All parents sometimes undermine their children with bad-tempered and inconsistent punishment, forgetting to tell them that they are appreciated, expecting unquestioning obedience or generally finding them a nuisance. But if children argue back and parents are reasonable enough to listen, the interchange can empower a child rather than dent her confidence.

Children who have lived in an atmosphere of criticism for a long time, who feel disliked and neglected by their peers, or are consistently compared unfavourably with their siblings are especially likely to have a negative view of themselves, generalizing from specific events to colour their perception of themselves, and preventing them achieving anything like their real potential.

A fascinating fact about learned helplessness

If you worry that your child may have a touch of negativity, ask yourself whether any of these examples sound familiar:

- The reasonable 'So and so is angry because I dropped a plate' is replaced by the unreasonable 'So and so hates me.'
- The reasonable 'So and so doesn't want to talk to me today' becomes 'Nobody wants me.'
- The reasonable 'This task is too difficult' turns into the unreasonable 'I'm stupid and useless.'

If your child has any of these tendencies, make sure you remind her which interpretation is true.

DO IT YOURSELF: How high is your self-esteem?

		Strongly agree	Agree	Disagree	Strongly disagree
1	I feel that I'm worth as much as other people.	☐	☐	☐	☐
2	I feel that I have a number of good qualities.	☐	☐	☐	☐
3	I am inclined to feel that I am a failure.	☐	☐	☐	☐
4	I am able to do things as well as most other people.	☐	☐	☐	☐
5	I feel I do not have much to be proud of.	☐	☐	☐	☐
6	I have a positive attitude towards myself.	☐	☐	☐	☐
7	On the whole, I am satisfied with myself.	☐	☐	☐	☐
8	I wish I could have more self-respect.	☐	☐	☐	☐
9	I feel useless at times.	☐	☐	☐	☐
10	At times I think I am no good at all.	☐	☐	☐	☐

Scoring:
Statements 1, 2, 4, 6, 7: score 3 for strongly agree, 2 for agree, 1 for disagree, 0 for strongly disagree.
Statements 3, 5, 8, 9, 10: score 0 for strongly agree, 1 for agree, 2 for disagree, 3 for strongly disagree.

Score 1–10: You have a rather low sense of self-worth.
Score 11–20: You're middle of the road.
Score 21–30: You have high self-esteem.

There is another way that children can lose self-belief and that is if their parents are so worried about the dangers of modern life they become over-protective. Children need to be allowed to do things on their own and to make their own mistakes. But, while some parents are so lax their children run wild, which can be dangerous, many of us have gradually become more protective of our children and less willing to allow them to develop independence. In some ways, over-protection can have a similar effect to being overly criticized: both reduce a child's ability to trust her instincts, her sense of agency is undermined and so is her self-belief.

As a five-year-old child I was able to play in the streets, and was sent off to the shops and school alone or in the company of my seven-year-old sister. I wasn't unusual. Even thirty years ago, young children went to the swimming pool on their own and scarcely ever saw a doctor. A recent survey shows just how much the freedom we took for granted thirty years ago has been curtailed.

Fascinating facts about worried parents

- Over half of mothers are now obsessed with their children's health, reporting high anxiety levels about mild colds and the possibility of choking on small objects.
- A quarter of mothers take their children to see the doctor every two or three months.
- Most worry about stranger danger, although in reality only a very tiny number of children are harmed by outsiders.
- Many are frightened if their children get near water or close to stairs.
- Two-thirds of mothers don't like their young children to walk – or run – on a pavement unless they are holding hands with an adult.
- Most children are not allowed out to play on their own until they are eleven years old.
- And yet a quarter of mothers confessed that they were worried their children did not get enough exercise.

Fear is catching, so it is worth thinking carefully about whether your fears are realistic. Some children genuinely can't be trusted near water or roads, some places are too dangerous to play in and some children are physically fragile, but is yours? Some parents don't give their children a chance to prove themselves. Over-protective parenting has a particularly pernicious knock-on effect for anxious or shy children. Unlike a robust, outgoing child who will break the rules and push for independence come what may, a naturally cautious child will have her fears confirmed by yours and will reject healthy autonomy for your peace of mind. Being able to trust that the outside world is safe and teeming with good people is important not just for you, but for her. Fortunately, self-belief can change for the better, as this next story can confirm.

THE UNATTRACTIVE STUDENT'S STORY

In the 1930s a group of young college men, psychologists in the making, were motivated by an unhealthy desire to play God, and targeted a dull, unattractive female student and subtly courted her. They professed to enjoy her company, admired her appearance and her mind, and escorted her to the most prestigious events in the college social calendar. The young woman enjoyed the attention; she dressed better and grew to like herself. She made new friends, she allowed herself to have opinions and make jokes. Gradually she became more lively and attractive. And then, one dreadful day, she discovered the truth. She wasn't liked for herself: she was her fellow students' guinea pig. History doesn't relate how she coped with this revelation, but cope she did. Her new self-belief and joy in life kept her afloat and she remained one of the more popular students of the year, and was able, even years later, to dine out on the story.

Self-esteem is not just something we are born with; it is made in large part by other people. And, as this story shows, self-belief can be moulded.

WHAT YOU CAN DO ... for all children

- First you need to look at your child's level of self-belief. If you think it is getting a bit dented, don't worry! Self-esteem can be boosted, but you need to take positive action. Parents, friends and teachers can transform your child's world.
- Ask yourself why she doesn't have high self-esteem. Is it because she is criticized a lot? A good rule of thumb is that you should show that you appreciate what your child does five times more often than you criticize her, or even more frequently if her self-esteem is down, and you shouldn't criticize and or shame her, especially in front of others.
- Is it because she is frightened and finds the world a bewildering place? Check to see if you are over-protecting her. Does she catch her fears from you? If so, can you let her off the rein? Or maybe she is naturally anxious and needs a bit of time out from all the choices and excitement out there. Try limiting her to straightforward either/or choices like 'Do you want to play with your dolls or with your Lego?', 'Do you want an apple or an orange?' In fact this is a good thing to do with every child; too many choices can be overwhelming.
- Anxious children, babies included, crave comfort and if you are clever you can use this to your – and her – advantage. The more

support you provide to help with specific anxieties, the more she'll grow to like herself. Sometimes children who start life anxious and uncertain can become the most confident of adults.

WHAT YOU CAN DO ... for babies

- Babies are too young to worry about what other people think, but that doesn't mean they can't feel bad about themselves. They can. Babies who are often left to cry can sometimes end up feeling worthless and will gradually turn away from their parents rather than look to them for help. Children who are comforted quickly feel good, and that feeling will contribute to the development of high self-esteem when they are older. So the most affirming thing you can do for your baby is to act quickly when she is sad, enjoy her when she is happy and comfort her whenever she needs you.

WHAT YOU CAN DO ... for toddlers

- Is she lacking in self-esteem because she doesn't feel loved or liked? Talk with her in a way that makes her feel good about herself. Discuss things with her, tell her you enjoy her company and spend as much quality time as you can with her.
- Does she feel that she always fails? Give her tasks that she can succeed in. Support her if she asks for help, but don't do it yourself. She needs you to reassure her and witness that she can do things, not take over and prove that she can't. And don't give in to the temptation of telling her it is easy. She knows that and telling her will just make it worse. It's only by succeeding that she will convince herself that she does have power and is worth believing in!

WHAT YOU CAN DO ... for older children

- Does your child use the three styles of thinking described earlier in this chapter? They are symptoms of fearfulness and you should always correct them. So if she says 'You don't love me,' tell her that you do. If she has broken something, tell her, 'I do love you, but I don't love that broken plate!'
- Does she have a specific problem? Perhaps she feels unattractive, academically slow or frustrated because she isn't very dextrous. You can tackle specific problems by giving targeted help – making sure she has the right clothes, helping her to read, or playing ball games – and by being extra diligent about appreciating her activities in the areas she feels more confident with.

How to Strengthen Resilience

The word 'resilient' was coined to describe a type of metal that ricochets back into its original shape whatever force it has been under. Resilient people do the same. Resilience doesn't prevent shock, suffering or disappointment, but it does enable a rapid bounce back. It's good for kids to get knocks, but only if they learn that they can survive them.

Resilient people learn well because they know they might get things wrong, and can handle whatever follows. Often, challenging circumstances can breed resilience. Difficult childhoods can break us, but they can also make us. The process is called 'stress inoculation', and those who develop immunity to disaster can become quite fearless and frequently very powerful.

Alison Lapper speaks

Alison was disabled from birth. In spite of her disability and rejection by her family early in life, she became an artist and was recently honoured with an MBE from the Queen, for her services to art. She became a public figure from the *Child of Our Time* TV shows and when a huge marble statue called *Alison Lapper, pregnant* by the British artist Marc Quinn was displayed in London's Trafalgar Square.

> *I'm someone who is happy most of the time and stubborn; I don't like people telling me what to do. I was brought up in a care home with other disabled children and couldn't move much when I was little. I was in artificial limbs that were heavy and uncomfortable and I felt trapped. Not only was I disabled, but I was dyslexic and called stupid as well. We weren't even allowed to go out much, because we upset the general public, which makes me laugh now because I love upsetting the general public!*

Stress inoculation is not unusual, but it is not the only progenitor of resilience. Long-term studies show how important it can be to know we are loved and supported when we are young. A secure, positive bond, the powerful attachment between adult and child, is the foundation on which resilience and confidence rests. It helps us become self-reliant and resourceful, and gives us a positive sense of self-worth, which in turn liberates us to get on with learning and having a good time. But resilience also depends on personality, and some of us are more vulnerable than others.

Gillian speaks

Gillian was bullied at school and left at fifteen to start work. It took ten years for her to find the confidence to take a law degree, but she still feels she has low self-esteem and setbacks still upset her.

> *I'm an out-and-out pessimist, very much a loner, and I think it's better to prepare yourself for the very, very worst that can happen. It's always been like that. I remember at school when we had to throw the shot and I thought I could do it and I put every bit of effort I had and it vanished and I thought 'This is wonderful, it must have gone for miles …' and then it landed at my feet, and the teacher came and told me to stop playing the goat. I try and put on a good front now and again, which is perhaps a mistake because people think I'm that sort of person, when underneath I'm just creeping around. You need something to help you cope with it because I think if you have confidence you can get on and be happy.*

When disaster strikes, unhappy children tend to remain upset for longer – the incident burns on, sometimes for ever, whereas happy children are more resilient and often forget about it, partly because of genetic influences that protect from a tendency to depression. Brain chemicals like serotonin (the chemical supplemented by modern anti-depressants) and endorphin (the brain's natural opiate) play a part in this.

ELIZA'S STORY

Eliza is a friend of mine, a sweet four-and-a-half-year-old girl with a highly developed sense of right and wrong. Just last week she went shopping for a birthday present with her mother, Sadie. Eliza loved the shop and finally chose the perfect present – a pink and green spotted piggy bank. But the china pig was smooth and too big for her small hands and as she tried to pick it up it slipped and crashed on to the floor, breaking into smithereens. Eliza bawled with shame and worry. Sadie suggested that Eliza could make amends by spending all her own money, amounting to £2, to pay for

the damage. The tears stopped, Eliza brightened and happily handed over the money. By the time she left the shop she was proud of the drama, and so she should have been. She knew she had done wrong, was delighted to put it right, and had learnt a good lesson – that disasters are rarely as bad as they seem. Just knowing that fact breeds resilience.

DO IT YOURSELF

You can find out how resilient your child is by watching what happens if something goes wrong. The sorts of situations that reveal resilience are:

- He drops something and it breaks
- Someone accidentally ruins his game
- A ball is thrown into the next-door garden and someone has to get it
- He gets a meal he doesn't like
- You all miss a train.

Does your child:

- Shrug it off immediately
- Look grumpy and cry but get over it quickly
- Cry inconsolably for some time or remain grumpy for the rest of the day?

Your child is resilient if he can shrug off disappointment and deal with the fall-out. Being grumpy or crying for a short time is quite normal, but watch out if he usually cries a lot and finds it hard to take remedial action.

The interaction between genes and environment is noticeable in very young babies. Some are born easygoing, others may be born more anxious. Anxious babies tend to find it hard to recover from painful events – from stomach aches to separation – and, if they are to build resilience, may need more help than easygoing babies. Paradoxically, difficult or anxious babies are easier to influence, perhaps because they demand so much more of your undivided attention, so treating them with consideration and understanding is especially effective.

Children who are less resilient tend to share particular traits:
- When things go wrong they usually think it is their fault – so if they spill some water it is because they are clumsy.
- When people are cross with them they usually think they have been bad.
- If they are disappointed they can't hide their feelings.
- If they can't manage a difficult task they feel that they are stupid.
- If they are criticized they take it to heart and find it hard to recover.
- If someone accidentally breaks their toy or damages something they were making they find it hard to start again.
- They often feel shame and guilt about things that are not their fault. For instance, if their parent breaks something they feel anxious and guilty.
- They may have a general feeling of anxiety.

Resilient children also tend to share particular traits:
- When things go wrong they usually think it is because of external issues – so if they spill some water on the floor it's because the cup was too full.
- When people are cross with them they usually think it is because of an accidental mishap, not a personality defect.
- If they are disappointed they can hide their feelings.
- If they can't manage a difficult task they think the task is too hard for them.
- If their parent breaks something they think it is funny.
- If they are criticized they shrug it off quickly.
- If someone accidentally breaks their toy or damages something they were making, they find it easy to start again.
- They rarely feel shame or guilt about things that are not their fault.
- They usually don't have a general feeling of anxiety.

Marie speaks

Marie is one of the most resilient people I have ever met. As a child, Marie had an extremely unsettled childhood. She moved schools seven times, her mother departed, leaving her in the care of her father, and eventually she went into care. But Marie's optimism is undimmed; she has educated herself and is now running her own business.

❝ I love having fun and I like going to work and spending time with the children. And I'm a strong person, so if I'm not happy in a situation then I have to do something about it. I have a fifteen-year plan and once the fifteen years are up I will have three properties in three countries. You can do anything that you want to do if you put your mind to it; you can achieve whatever you want to. One of the things my daughter, Tanesha, said to me when she was little was that she wanted to be a dustman. I said 'That's great, go and be a dustman, but own the company!' ❞

WHAT YOU CAN DO ... for all children

- Praise their resilience! You can watch how your child behaves when there is an upset and praise his ability to bounce back from the very start. This has a twofold benefit: you always know how resilient he is feeling, and, because your child wants to please you, he will try to do what you want.
- Talk positively to your child much more often than you criticize his actions. And make it a rule to refute any of his negative core beliefs (see p.87). He will feel much safer if he knows you don't mind accidents and that you firmly believe he's a good kid who does his best.
- Your child will do things that annoy you, lots of things! But if you believe in him, then if there is a mishap, you will comfort him rather than face him angrily. Why? Because angry parents frighten children and frightened children don't learn resilience, they learn to panic.

WHAT YOU CAN DO ... for babies

- Now is the time to start praising effort, helping your baby as needed and reassuring him that it's good to experiment. And if your baby is upset and you comfort him he will begin to realize that the world is a safe place and there are people he can rely on. This is an essential start to developing resilience.
- Some babies are naturally anxious and will need more reassurance from you when they are very young. Don't worry – give it to them and they'll thrive.

WHAT YOU CAN DO ... for toddlers

- Young children are very egotistical, unable to envisage a world that doesn't revolve around them. As a result they are likely to believe that whatever happens is their fault, from their sibling breaking something to divorce or death in the family. This tendency can be exacerbated at around three, when children start to feel shame and guilt. Spot when your child hasn't got things in perspective and check he's not carrying other people's problems that sap his resilience.
- Children love to play with their parents. Alas, lots of parents don't love to play with their children, but it is worth setting time aside to be with them. Pick games you will both enjoy – drawing, football, cooking, it doesn't much matter what – and set out to have a good time.

Katy speaks

"" *Last week my mum was obsessed with Happy Families. We had this rule that we had to give back the card we'd won if we didn't say 'Thank you' when we got it. Mum thought it was great and my little sister did too. She loved it and she's only four! But I was nearly the best, because I'm seven, though Dad won in the end. It was fun.* ""

WHAT YOU CAN DO ... for older children

- Older children build resilience through knowing that failure brings sympathy not retribution. Resilient children can manage a great deal of healthy competition, happily trying to win and, equally, accepting failure – in fact they use failure to increase motivation. Children who are less independent and more proud may need you to demonstrate clearly how little failure matters, helping them to recognize successes and pointing out that everyone, including yourself, fails sometimes. If you can persuade your child to see his failures as tools for learning then you really have hit the jackpot!

How to Develop Concentration

If your child learns to concentrate single-mindedly, she will become immeasurably powerful. If concentration is combined with persistence, success is almost guaranteed.

Concentration is essentially a solitary, internal state of mind, when the world and its worries disappear and what you are doing is the only thing that counts. This feeling of being totally engaged, to the exclusion of everything else, is called 'flow'. Flow not only gives us a short-term buzz, it also gives us long-term fulfilment.

Everyone concentrates for a short time – it's very difficult not to focus on one thing or another – but if we can stay with a task until it is finished we are lucky, because a focussed mind can achieve a great deal in a very short time.

DO IT YOURSELF

All babies concentrate – that's how they learn.

Two-to-three-month-old babies love a challenge and will focus intently in order to solve problems. Learning how to move a noisy mobile is one challenge that my daughter loved.

Hang bells on a mobile fixed above your baby's cot or chair. Fix a soft ribbon to the mobile and tie the other end loosely around her leg and leave her to it. Sooner or later she will discover that when she kicks her leg the mobile moves and bells ring. She'll want to check out how it happened, and step by step she'll work out the mechanism. She'll try moving her leg slowly and quickly, exploring the different rhythms of the bells and the wild or gentle movements of the mobile. This game can last for a long time, but when she has exhausted the possibilities of this set-up, try tying the ribbon loosely on to her arm and see how long it takes for her to recognize that she needs to stop kicking her leg and start waving her arm. This concentrated experience, where your child uses all her brain power, will give her a great deal of pleasure.

You can invent other games for your baby, your toddler and your older child. If you play into their interests and pitch challenges at the right level for them, they are likely to enjoy them enormously.

My young daughter set about doing things as if she was asking questions. She would clatter a couple of saucepans and lids with an expression of intense concentration. 'Can I lift it? Can I lift and turn it at the same time? What happens if I bang it down on the ground? Will it fit inside?'and so on. Like all children, she didn't need to know the 'right' way to use a pan, she just wanted answers to the hundreds of questions she had about weight, shape, noise and her own strength. If you distract a child who is concentrating, she might get cross or you might see her go back to her own line of reasoning as soon as you turn your back. Whichever she does, you risk breaking her line of thought. And concentration is very mood enhancing; a child who can concentrate at fifteen months is likely to be happier at nursery at three or four, even if she has a rather anxious personality and is prone to be overwhelmed by new situations. Indeed, I have often noticed that shyness and good concentration seem to go together, as if one compensates for the other. But for all of us, the ability to focus on a single task is extremely important.

DO IT YOURSELF

Adults also enjoy concentrating. Some parents from the *Child of Our Time* project told us about their recent experiences of 'flow':

Andy:	When I go out on my motorbike.
Debbie:	Doing all sorts of sports and fitness.
Jonathan:	On a river, fishing.
Helen:	Well, I laid some laminate floor at the weekend and it was a challenge but I could not stop until it was all done and I just went on for hours and it was brilliant!

When was the last time you had 'flow'? How often do you get it? Once a day? Once a week? Once a month? And what about your children? Do

they get 'flow' easily and often? What gives them their most concentrated experiences? Are they active or passive? Or do they struggle to find the time or energy to become totally absorbed in what they are doing?

The *Child of Our Time* children were given a flow-inducing experience – they were asked to conduct a small jazz band! Most of them loved the combination of being in charge, experimenting with speed and rhythm and being totally immersed in the situation. Some of them got so into it, they had to be dragged away so the others could have a turn.

Concentration is controlled, at least in part, by our genes. There are specific regions of the brain which are responsible for how well we concentrate, and these differ in size and complexity from one individual to the next. While many children love to concentrate and resent being interrupted, others find it very hard to focus on anything for a long time; in fact, the length of time that children can concentrate for varies enormously, from several hours to just a few minutes.

A fascinating fact about concentration and gender

Boys' senses are generally less acute than girls'. They don't hear as well and their sense of smell is less developed. Only their eyesight is as good. Inside their brains, boys have other differences and one of these is concentration. Some boys concentrate less well than girls, and there is a reason for this. The ability to concentrate may be loosely linked with genes and particularly with the sex-linked chromosomes X and Y. Females have two X chromosomes, so if they have genes on one that aren't ideal, the other can often make up for it. But males have just one X and a short Y chromosome, which carries instructions about being male. Some boys may get a less than perfect X chromosome alongside an active Y, and they don't have another X to compensate. Thus males can sometimes find it harder to concentrate than females.

One important skill, if you are to focus properly, is to work out what you need to do and block out the rest. We are all able to ignore some potentially distracting things – even babies can ignore background noises like traffic and the hum of computers. But many of us are hopeless at ignoring more attractive distractions.

DO IT YOURSELF

Test your mind control. Can you focus on the task in hand without being distracted by other powerful cues? You will need coloured pens and paper.

Ask a friend to write the names of lots of colours using different-coloured pens. For instance, they could write 'green' using a yellow pen. Each word should be written on a different piece of paper. Make about twelve of these and ask them to hold up each word in turn.

You have to say the colour it is written in as quickly as possible.

Do you say the colour or the word? A tricky switching of attention is required to say the colour, because most adults automatically register the word before the colour.

This test is called the Stroop Test after its inventor. If you are to succeed you will have to go slow, to allow your colour spotting to catch up with your reading. A few lucky people are very good at resisting the lure of words, but most of us take about twice as long to name the colour as to read the word.

Can your child focus on the task in hand without being distracted by other powerful cues? Scientists have done an experiment to test young children's ability to disregard distracting cues using pictures where an animal's body is attached to a different animal's head. For instance, a pig with a sheep's head, or a duck with a horse's head.

You could try this yourself by drawing – or downloading – pictures of seven or eight animals and pasting the heads on to different bodies, then asking your child to name each body as quickly as possible. The head is just there to distract him!

The faster and more accurate your child is in naming the body, the less distractible he is. Slower and less accurate children are more distractible. We did this test with the *Child of Our Time* children at the age of four. Some of them didn't get any right, but they all giggled a lot!

We tested adults and children by giving them a tricky task and setting up a comic distraction – a panda doing funny things on the balcony. Half the adults and two-thirds of the children were so distracted they failed to finish the task.

There is another mechanism at work in some children who lose concentration easily. We all need some excitement in our lives, but what if your metabolism is such that it takes something really frightening to give you half the adrenaline rush that other people get from going for a walk? There seems to be a huge variation between the level of difficulty and danger a person experiences in any given situation. Those of us who need a lot of stimulation will respond more to distractions, simply because life becomes intolerably dull without them. This is exacerbated in people with ADHD (attention-deficit hyperactivity disorder), who tend to seek very high levels of stimulation because they are not easily excited, which is why they are medicated not with a sedative, but with a stimulant.

There aren't many games that hold the long-term attention of children who find it harder to concentrate, but video games do.

Video games can be fun and challenging, and children who play them regularly develop quick reactions, good peripheral vision, and information-processing skills that, in an adept four-year-old, can rival those of any teenager or adult. Children also have to learn not to be distracted by anything irrelevant on screen if they are to be successful.

All these are good transferable skills that will support other activities. But there is a downside. Children – and adults – stay with the games for so long because they literally get stuck, induced to go on playing by a stream of rewards; where each move, each gold piece gained or figure blown up leads to the next in an endless cycle of adrenaline-fuelled excitement. And when a child who loves video games emerges dazed after a long session, other more laborious learning may seem ineffably boring. There is a danger that children who play a lot of video games may sometimes find it even harder to concentrate on things like important school work, simply because they are not being offered frequent rewards or getting the same 'buzz'. The answer is perhaps to limit video games; but it is also important to make other activities much more rewarding.

TOM AND TOBY'S STORY

It all started with a huge roll of thick wire which six-year-old Toby fell over, half buried as it was, in a field outside the house one sunny April afternoon. Toby's uncle, Tom, was also wandering across the field and Toby ran to him, shouting about his exciting find. Tom didn't think much of it at first sight, but, at the time, he was writing a book about the Norman invasion of Britain in 1066. No doubt this was in his mind when, five minutes later, he thought up the greatest game of the Easter holidays.

Tom sent Toby off to get some wire-cutters, some old sheets and lots of paint. Then they set about making the frame of a huge Norman soldier. They cut bits of metal to make his armour, they used a colander for a helmet and felt-tip pens to colour the sheets that formed the soldier's body and head. Huge black eyes and an angry red mouth were pinned on, a gesticulating arm carrying a big heavy sword was put in place and Toby went to bed to dream of knights and blazing armies. And, finally, there was the soldier the next morning, ten foot high and standing firm in the breeze, a fierce warrior and a worthy foe.

Tom and Toby were planning to avenge the Battle of Hastings. But first they needed weapons. Five-foot-long, tough, flexible sticks were cut from a willow tree and stringed to make far-reaching bows. Shorter pieces of elder, tipped with bent wire, became arrows, and the fun began.

It was a perfect weekend for a child whose concentration was always fleeting. Each exciting step in the construction opened new possibilities. And when the soldier was complete, there was the challenge of making and using the unfamiliar bow, and the rewarding sense of achievement for every on-target shot.

Well after dark, when the adults were sitting round the dining-room table, they could still hear the metallic twang of Toby's arrows hitting the Norman soldier, and his whoops of delight when he got him in the heart.

WHAT YOU CAN DO ... for all children

- 'PARENTS KEEP OUT' is written on thousands of children's doors all over the world. And why is that? Because children know from long experience that parents are always interrupting and they don't like it! Children of all ages need uninterrupted time to get really stuck in to an activity. That way they learn what concentration means, and the rewards of productive activity make them want to do more. It's a virtuous circle that we can all relate to.

- Some children will stick with one task; others flit from thing to thing. Neither of these styles is wrong, but being able to stay focused on one task is going to be important for school work. Although genes play a part, being able to concentrate is also a skill that can be fostered. Find something your child is really interested in, give her the tools to get going – including your time – and let her take her own path. She may stick at it for hours, or she may be distracted, come back, be distracted and eventually finish days later. If she does the latter, you mustn't clear up! Let her keep several activities on the go and she'll find out how rewarding it is to finish things. Tidy them away and she'll never gain this vital knowledge.

A fascinating fact about diet and concentration

Fish oils are well known to help the nervous system settle and to improve concentration, and are sold by the bucket load from pharmacies and supermarkets. But who is helped by the fish oils, omega 3, 6 and 9, and why might they work? Tests show that omega oils are vital to build a healthy nervous system because they speed up the transmission of information along nerves and in the brain. Paradoxically, however, the vast majority of fish-oil consumers are middle class, have a balanced diet, no omega oil deficit, and no problems with concentration, while more deprived children with a poor diet rarely take omega oil supplements because they are too expensive and also because these groups often don't believe in their efficacy. Scientists still have a long way to go in correcting that inequality!

WHAT YOU CAN DO ... for babies

• Your baby loves challenges and adores making things happen, especially when you can offer a rich environment. Watch how she works things out and when she's had enough, and why – is the activity too easy for her, or too difficult? Adjust the activity until it is challenging but do-able and see how much more readily she practises her talent for concentration.

WHAT YOU CAN DO ... for toddlers

• Toddlers are infinitely curious and determined to explore the world. While forcing your child to do something she's evidently not interested in will be counter-productive, if not impossible, enjoying her company and showing her things that keep her interest as long as possible is well worth the effort. She'll have fun and you'll have the pleasure of knowing that she's learning about the world around her.

WHAT YOU CAN DO ... for older children

• Older children also enjoy challenges, so create them, providing just enough help to enable your child to keep at it until she's succeeded. However well she concentrates, if the activity takes a long time it's worth taking breaks, for food, exercise or just a bit of quiet time. If you help to keep her aspiration in mind, she'll come back refreshed and ready to finish later.

• Older children who are less good at concentrating need a powerful reason to stick with a piece of work – or play. Children like this learn faster if they learn little and often. Try planning each step with your child and keep on top of how much has been done. It can be more effective to alternate work and breaks; if your child is enjoying herself, she will want to get back to the task and if she scents success she will eventually get it done.

How to Deal with Laziness

Children are supreme strategists. If they can get you to work for them, they will, and if you don't prevent it, will come to believe it is their right. Then they get lazy and laziness is the enemy of learning.

JAVAN'S STORY

Javan was brought up in a small house at the edge of a big city. A much-wanted child, he was distanced by age from his teenage step-brother, and by the time he was two his mother and father, though still living together, were drifting noisily apart. Javan's mother, Anna, doted on her second son. As a baby, he was cheerful and startlingly beauliful and Anna bathed in the glory. He was her comfort when things got bad, her excuse for shopping and her main occupation. And, like all mothers, Anna wanted to keep him safe. But what she did was far from that. When Javan was four, Anna had still not taught him how to dress himself; he wasn't allowed to choose his games or his clothes, nor was he given challenging toys. Anna, through love, had kept him totally dependent, telling him that things were too difficult or too dangerous, wanting him to be the glorious baby she used to have. But Javan wasn't glorious. He was frustrated and often bored; he had nightmares, and clung to Anna like glue.

The day came for him to start school. He cried, and so did she. Two weeks later Anna's husband finally departed, and Anna was left with very little. She had no option but to look for work and when she got it, found herself overstretched for the first time. This was her opportunity and Javan's. Necessity could have propelled Javan into tidying his toys and learning how to look after himself, but Anna was consumed by guilt and did not want Javan to have to pay for her misfortune. And, of course, she was tired, and persuading her son out of his inactivity would be a struggle. So Javan was left to his own devices; he became a computer whiz, and spent a lot of time dreaming in his room.

At sixteen, imbued with passivity since birth, Javan is a big, bored boy, with a good heart, a growing waistband, and no wish to move from his comfortable home. Someone, he feels, will always be there to look after him. Sometime he might have to take responsibility, but no one is holding their breath.

Laziness isn't always a moral defect, a strategic response designed to get other people to do all the work. I know of several children whose laziness is really due to feeling not respected by family, carers, teachers or peers. So what sort of feelings cause laziness?

- Children can be less proactive if they feel that anything they do might turn out to be wrong. I've often seen families whose children become the butt of their jokes and experience a wearing repetition of humiliating stories cloaked as comedy that can drain the life out of them. In my experience this is usually linked to the parents' own lack of ambition, but in such circumstances, children are quick to find that it's not worth putting themselves out.

- Older children can be deeply discouraged by demands that can't be met. Often such demands come from outside the family. For instance, they may get depressed about school work, about not having the 'right' possessions, or they may be ashamed of their home life. These worries can be very demotivating, because whatever they do doesn't seem to gain them the respect they badly need.

- Physical punishment is an important issue for children and tends to discourage proactive behaviour. According to one study, over 90 per cent of children have been hit at some time in their lives and over half are smacked at least once a week. Most child-rearing experts believe that anything more than a light tap is morally dubious, practically ineffective, extremely demotivating, and potentially dangerous.

- Tiredness, insufficient good food, or illness will also cause a child to feel drained and lazy. Low physical energy is also due to not getting enough sleep, and is especially common in children who have a TV or games console in their bedroom. So it can often be dealt with fairly simply by removing the TV, if parents can stomach a battle.

Behind these routes to laziness lies the same fundamental issue – children who, for one reason or another, do not feel responsible for their own lives. But there is one sort of so-called 'laziness' that isn't laziness at all. It occurs when children don't want to do what their parents want them to.

JOSH'S STORY

I know a keen and loving father who, years after the event, talks ruefully about how he tried to get his young son, Josh, to share his passion for cars. In the beginning it went well. I remember walking down the road with Josh when he was only one; I pointed out a car. 'Car,' I said to him. He looked at me with derision and said 'BMW'. He was right, already way ahead of me in the I-Spy cars stakes. But by the time he was four he had totally turned off the subject. For him car talk had become mere noise. And the reason? One weekend his father had taken him to a car museum, followed by a complete service of their own old, recalcitrant VW van. Josh's childish interest began to wane in the face of incomprehensible explanations in the museum, and died when his dad, Alec, insisted he 'helped' with the service, which was cold and boring. So when Alec suggested he came out on another car expedition, Josh told his father he preferred to watch TV. This happened more than once and Alec reached the conclusion that Josh, now only five, was lazy, and proclaimed he was getting to be 'like a teenager'. But Josh wasn't. He just didn't like cars, and he didn't like being told that he should.

Over the years I have found that it's quite common for parents to feel let down when their children don't share their interests, and their irritation encourages them to label their child lazy, rather than respecting, albeit regretfully, that he has his own valid likes and dislikes. Switching off through boredom may look like laziness, but canny parents can find that it isn't by examining their child's current passions. There will be some, and their child will probably be highly motivated in this respect, but children may keep parents in the dark because they know they won't want to join in. After all, why should a parent love the intracies of dolls' clothes or want to spend hours in an uncomfortable den under the bed? Family peace is a lot easier to maintain if you respect your child's choices most of the time in return for him gracefully taking part in your favourite outings when he has to.

WHAT YOU CAN DO ... for all children

- There is one force of nature you can use as much as you want and that is the universal desire of children for attention, so attend to your child's passions and show your appreciation when he gets interested in an activity.
- Try to be aware of signs that your child is running away from responsibility and see if you can work out when and why, and if there are root causes that you can help with. The quicker you act, the less entrenched he will become.
- Trust your child, believe in him. If you don't, he won't.
- Don't use physical punishment and always try to be fair.
- Use the power of talk to get him motivated.
- Make sure he gets enough good food and plenty of sleep.
- And remember that children need to feel both safe and challenged, balanced between your boundaries and taking responsibility for themselves. They love knowing where they stand, and if they push the limits, it's usually because they want to take more responsibility, something that should give you pleasure!

WHAT YOU CAN DO ... for babies

- Your baby is never lazy! Babies have to learn and they do. Parents who think they have a lazy baby probably just have a child who is naturally phlegmatic, and the only danger here is that parents might not give him the stimulation that more anxious children demand as a matter of right. So if you are lucky enough to have a good-natured baby, just remember that, though he might not shout for it, he will thrive if he gets as much attention and play time as more fractious children.

WHAT YOU CAN DO ... for toddlers

- Toddlers often try their parents' patience, but they are only experimenting and as a result getting lots of great experience. Your toddler will flourish, especially if you get into the habit of giving him concentrated help to find and enjoy stimulating new activities when he is bored.
- Reinforce his sense of agency by saying what you see – 'I see you

enjoyed making that castle' – and by offering things that move him on – 'You like playing with bricks so I have brought you something extra to use.'

- Your child will love having responsibility for small jobs: to hang up his coat, lay the table and 'look after' his little sibling, and these little things are important, the first steps towards becoming a responsible member of society.

WHAT YOU CAN DO ... for older children

- If your child seems lazy and discouraged, there are effective motivational tools you can use to help.
- Your job now is to admire what he does and encourage him.
- He is likely to benefit greatly if you give him some responsibility for the running of the household. If it's difficult to motivate him to do chores then you can use a technique that involves choices. For instance, if he won't lay the table, ask him if he will do the washing-up instead. If that's a problem, explain why you need his help and find out what ideas he has about how to solve the impasse. Children are usually very good at generating solutions as long as the conversations are easygoing – getting angry is not a good route! And, of course, when he does his jobs (even if they are initially slow or slap-dash) don't forget to appreciate his efforts.
- The good news is that when your child regains power it will be enormously self-affirming. Someone who manages to get their self-esteem back, taking responsibility and recognizing the efficacy of his own efforts, feels great. It's a positive cycle and the more powerful you feel, the better.

DO IT YOURSELF

Reaching into a discouraged child's world can be immensely rewarding. One way is to ask him to take photographs. Try suggesting that he looks for his five favourite things, his best places and his most loved people. Also suggest that he photographs the things he doesn't like, and the spaces where he is most frightened (he may need you to accompany him!). Talking about these photos together will give you a unique understanding of how your child's emotions impact on the rest of his life.

The Child of Our Time *children's photos of their favourite things ranged from birds to their classroom.*

Over time I have met many unhappy children with disappointed parents and despairing lives. Luckily I have met many more happy, confident young people who imagine the future as rosy and themselves as indestructible. The endgame is clear: all the parents I have ever spoken to want their children to become happy, motivated adults. Children want that too, and the key is to give your children respect and responsibility.

DO IT YOURSELF

If your child feels helpless and unmotivated, try having a day when ...

- You ask his advice on what to do (for instance, when to have lunch and what to eat) at least five times in the day, and always take it with pleasure.
- You show him joyfully how to do something new and don't leave him floundering.
- You never say 'Yes, but ... it won't work' and always say 'Yes, that would be fun.'
- You never say 'Well done,' and always say 'I saw you do that and I thought ...'
- You never take decisions he can take for himself, and always appreciate his (even if he decides to wear his scruffiest clothes).
- You never say 'No' (unless he is in danger) and always say 'Yes' (though sometimes it will be 'After I have finished ...').
- You never tell him what he is feeling and always repeat back to him what he says to you about his feelings.
- You never criticize but try to make him smile instead.
- You listen to yourself talking to your child and really think about the effects of what you say.

Make a note of what worked, and stick it somewhere prominent to remind you to do it again.

Praising effectively, nurturing confidence, concentration and resilience and tackling laziness can, with love and patience, raise the game of any child and overturn even the most stubborn case of demotivation. It is said that once this reversal has happened a few times, we learn an opposite lesson: we know we can survive and we may even begin to feel invincible.

PART THREE
REMEMBER?

Human memory beggars belief. No one knows how much information any one person can remember because it has proved impossible to find a limit. The seemingly infinite capacity to learn is just beginning when we are born.

CHARLIE'S STORY

Charlie was born on 14 January 2000, a perfect baby girl. Four women were there when she made her entry into the new millennium: her mother Toni, only seventeen years old, her grandmother Anne, her great-grandmother Barbara and great-great-grandmother Kate. Of gypsy heritage, they supposedly carried a curse that prophesied a line of girls, and Charlie was a girl, so all was as it should be.

But as Charlie cried and opened her eyes, what did she see? Did she feel connected to these four loving women? How long would it take her to learn about them? Did she have any inkling that the world she was born into would be very different to her mother's, let alone her great-great-grandmother's?

Imagine yourself without a past or a future. What would it be like if you couldn't recall what happened a minute ago or envisage what you might do in the next minute? How would you feel? Imagine how intensely you would experience everything that happened, totally immersed in what you saw, felt or heard as though it was the very first time such things had ever occurred. And what about if something went wrong? How would you know it was wrong and what would you feel if you didn't know it might stop?

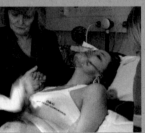

Charlie was like this, as are all babies. Without conscious memory, she arrived in a world that consisted of a series of unrelated moments. She heard herself crying, acutely aware of being miserable, only to forget as soon as she was comforted. And at that precious moment of birth, Charlie saw all four motherly women, but when they turned away to talk they were gone and no image remained. For her they ceased to exist, and their absence, like their presence, felt like eternity.

Even so, Charlie was already beginning to know things that even great-great-grandmother Kate baulked at. The hum of machinery and the speed of modern life would soon be as familiar to her as the movement of night to day.

Memory is more than the recall of facts. What we know makes us who we are. We remember things that make us happy, miserable times come back to haunt us without our volition and we cannot shrug them off, yet we forget the names of our friends. We spend hours learning facts that disappear in exam conditions, but many years ago, before writing was commonplace, people memorized huge amounts of information and could repeat it at will. Now, as much as ever, knowledge is power, informing our thinking and enlivening our conversation. So how can we train a good memory?

Memories are made by a truly amazing process that takes information from short-term memory, which sieves and chunks information, and moves it into long-term memory, the storehouse of everything we know. Active working memory is linked to short-term memory, but is much less passive; it is where we think, combining things we're experiencing now with ideas and information taken out of long-term storage.

This section is about how to remember and what to do if remembering is difficult. In it I shall show you how to teach your children not to rely solely on the internet, but to store memories and knowledge in the only place where they can really use it – their own brain. But first, what is memory and how does it develop?

Memory Basics

If your child is to know the world, she has to learn to remember. Without memory we are nothing. Fortunately your baby starts to store information as soon as her brain is capable. First she will remember the people she sees and hears, then she will start to imitate movements and, very gradually, her long-term memory will start to fill until she can put down memories accurately and retrieve them at will. What your child remembers, and, crucially, the context in which she remembers them, will shape her mind and influence her thinking.

Fascinating facts about the development of memory

- Even before she is born, your child can recognize things like her mother's voice and music, as I discovered when we tested the *Child of Our Time* newborns and found they responded to songs they had heard many times in the womb by relaxing happily. But at this age your child will not be able to recall one-off events.
- At two months, tests have shown that babies can remember an event for two or three days if reminded of it, but will still be unable to recall it at will.
- At one year, your child can remember a person or event for several months and now she can recall some one-off events. We know this because she can copy things she has once seen on TV – a dance, for instance. But one-year-olds tend only to remember the 'how', not the when, where or who with. So she will remember how to dig a hole but not who taught her.
- At two years she can remember who did what and when, and, depending how precocious her language is, will begin to recount what has happened during her day. Few adults remember events from this time, so she will probably forget them too.
- At three years she will use language as a tool for remembering and will categorize memories more effectively so her ability to recall becomes faster and more accurate.
- At four years she will be able to organize her thoughts better, she will use rote learning more effectively and will know when

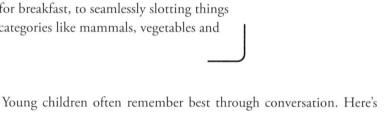

she has forgotten something. But she is still likely to get muddled. Her short-term memory bank is still small, which means that she can't hold as many facts in her mind as adults, and her use of memory-enhancing strategies is limited.

- At five years she has a bigger knowledge base and is developing a clearer memory as newly stored information links to the old.
- At six years she is well versed in the art of rehearsal. At this age many children consciously try to remember things by testing themselves over several days.
- At seven years old she is able to revel in free recall, calling up answers in response to questions because she has more explicit category links; if you listen to her you will probably notice that she is moving from thinking about particular things, like what's for breakfast, to seamlessly slotting things into more general categories like mammals, vegetables and geometric figures.

Young children often remember best through conversation. Here's one example from my friend Sadie, talking to her three-year-old daughter, Eliza.

Sadie:	We went to the seaside with Grandma and Grandpa. What did we do?
Eliza:	We made a sandcastle!
Sadie:	What did we use to make it?
Eliza:	My red bucket!
Sadie:	Yes, you had your red bucket. What did you collect in it?
Eliza:	Got some shells … and seaweed.
Sadie:	What did you do with them? Put them on top of the sandcastle? Then what happened?
Eliza:	*(jumping up and down in excitement)*: It fell down!
Sadie:	Yes, the tide came in and knocked the castle down and then we had our pasties.

Salience, importance, context, location, repetition, use of all senses, novelty and frequent recall all help cement memories. But by far the most powerful factor is when an event is imbued with emotion, and while love and laughter make for happy memories, the most enduring memories are those triggered by fear. Most of us have had an experience so burnt into our brain that we shy away from it for ever. It is very difficult to face eating or drinking something that has once made us ill, and for children who generalize faster than adults, a single traumatic experience can be so visceral it may create a phobia.

DAN'S STORY

Dan was a curious little boy who couldn't leave anything alone, until he met his nemesis in the shape of a small dog called Jumper. Jumper belonged to a neighbour. Like his master, he was an aggressive, irritable creature, growling and making to attack whenever he saw a stranger approaching. He was, in fact, a first-rate guard dog, trained to deter intruders. But young Dan didn't know this; he liked dogs and, true to his curious nature, he went to make friends. Imagine his fright when Jumper turned on him. Dan ran screaming back to his mother and after that he refused to go anywhere near Jumper. This was sensible, but like most children, Dan was quick to shift from the specific to the general. A few days after his encounter with Jumper, Dan refused to visit his grandmother because she had a dog. He was so upset, his parents agreed. Unbeknownst to them, Dan took this to mean that all dogs were dangerous and became convinced that it was safer to travel by car in case he met any dogs en route. By now Dan had developed a full-blown phobia, making his family's life a misery. Taking advice from a psychologist, they began to bring dogs back into Dan's life, starting with stories and ending with taking Dan kicking and screaming to his grandmother's house, where they first persuaded him to be in the same room as her dog, and then to touch it. Nothing scary happened and, as is often the case with children's phobias, Dan's fear soon dissipated and eventually disappeared. But Dan's phobia did not need to have gone so far. His parents belatedly realized that acting quickly would have been much more effective than letting him imagine so much, and fear so unnecessarily.

Emotions are the most powerful and uncontrollable of all the factors involved in memory and this is one reason why everyone's memory is uniquely theirs. Each person's memory bank is constructed from the experiences we have and the order they come in, overlaid by our interpretation of their meaning.

Memorizing with Your Senses

We saw on p.15 that learning is enhanced if we use all our senses. Recall is, too. Babies need to use all their senses to recognize a familiar situation, linking sight with colours, tastes, smells and sounds to drive it into their memory. Later they discover which of these elements is most important and become more focused on an object or action experienced through a single sense.

But remembering events without using all your senses has a downside: they become less easy to recall, which is why rhymes are more memorable than plain sentences, and rhymes put to music are even better. Some people cultivate multi-sensory links, learning to memorize poetry, for instance, by evoking pictures. And just a few extraordinary people can't help doing it. They have a syndrome called synaesthesia which can boost memory a lot, as I found out when my team filmed an exceptional man called James.

A DAY IN THE LAB

James has a very unusual life, as we found out when we visited him in the British town of Leicester.

First our researcher put on a CD of a Mozart horn concerto.

James: *'I'm getting short Coca Cola flavours, all sweet with Wine Gums. Now I can taste pineapple chunks. I like the gaps in the music because I get a load of chocolate thrown in. It's lovely! I'm even getting the temperature of the food, so it's a whole tasting experience.'*
For James it's not just music but words that trigger his synaesthesia.

'Monday tastes like a rubber band and on Tuesday I get the flavour of Opal Fruits through the entire day. Wednesday has a cake-like flavour. Thursday I get absolutely nothing. Friday is Spam, very strong Spam. Saturday it is bacon and Sunday is very cold orange juice. It's bizarre!'

This extraordinary aptitude has been good for James's memory.

'Synaesthesia has given me a passion for learning new words. If there's a word and I think "Oh, that tastes beautiful" I'll start using it. At school I got on really well with German, I loved it; it gave me a delicious marmalade flavour. And the German I learnt has stayed with me word for word.'

So James has learnt a lot because the taste of words makes them stick in his mind. But there is a downside. James is a pub landlord …

'Every evening I have to force myself to go into the front bar because I know so many people there. Names become a flavour as well as a person. And I'm thinking "Oh, he's a jam sandwich!" There's one there who is a Marmite sandwich. And I get processed peas, tinned carrots, burgers, fish fingers. I can't take the mix. Sometimes it makes me feel quite sick.'

At this point James had to leave the bar for a few moments to collect himself!

Conjuring up tastes in response to hearing a word is unusual, but the ability to use several senses is not, although it sometimes requires practice.

WHAT YOU CAN DO ... for all children

- Using all senses:
  Encourage your child to describe whatever she wants to remember in words, to whisper it under her breath.
  Encourage her to visualize it: ask her to describe it in pictures.
  Encourage her to make a connection between an object's name and the smell, place and people associated with it.

- It's much easier to remember things that stand out, that are unusual or a break from the routine, so make your outings and your home life exciting.
- Children remember better if they are aware of the context – the location, who was there, the smell, noise, taste or feel and what they were wearing and doing. We all rely on learning by association to keep our memories intact, and encouraging your child to notice the context will help to cement her memories.
- Children remember something more clearly when it happens for the first time – it's called the primacy effect. So give her lots of new experiences and help her revel in them both during and after the event.
- Your child will remember things that she believes are important, especially if they are imbued with emotion. In fact, once we move into the realms of emotion and experience, we can lose conscious control. So let her know how you feel if something is important to you and remind her of her emotional take on those events you would like her to recall.
- Your child is not only learning facts, she's learning 'how to ...' skills. Even our muscles have memory, which means that useful skills become automatic with practice, so encourage her to be active and to practise until the movements are imprinted into her body.
- Most importantly, memory is not an art but a science and benefits from repetition. Little and often is the rule – if your child gets a fact wrong, shorten the delay before repeating it, and then gradually extend it until the fact is learnt. This method is effective because, if you time it well, your child will get the answer right more often than wrong, and that's very motivating. A scientist called Ulric Neisser heard about this regime and was so pleased with it he produced a limerick:

> *You can get a good deal from rehearsal*
> *If it just has the proper dispersal*
> *You would just be an ass to do it en masse,*
> *Your remembering would turn out much worse!*

Active Memory

We hold a universe of things in our long-term memory and we juggle many bits of information in our active working memory, but all of it has to be funnelled through a tiny space in our brain that can only retain seven items at any one time, and then only for two seconds. This extraordinary portal into our long-term memory is called, prosaically, 'short-term memory'.

Short-Term Memory

Short-term memory really is short, both in the sense of being temporary – information is kept for about two seconds unless it is refreshed – and because it has very little capacity – it is kept alive by sending electric currents round a limited network of nerves.

DO IT YOURSELF

- Short-term memory is measured by asking people to remember random numbers, letters or objects.
- Scan the following letters quickly, look away and see how many you remember.

PHBDITCBRHTC

- Adults rarely remember more than seven letters and frequently just five or six.
- Try it with your child.
- Children score less. Four-year-olds' short-term memory will only take two to four items, five-year-olds' take five items and even nine-year-olds may only score six.
  But what happens if you look at the letters now?

PHD HRT BBC ICT

Though short-term memory can only manage about seven items at once, if we split the information into meaningful chunks we are left with just four easy concepts.

Short-term memory plays an extremely important role. It is here that our experiences – what we see, hear, understand and think – are sieved for usefulness and discarded in milliseconds if not needed, to let more information in for judgement. It exercises quality control, the filter that prevents us remembering a car in the background or passers-by on the street. What we do remember are those things we pay attention to.

Attention is very important for two reasons. Just as the things we pay attention to are the things we remember, conversely, I have always been astonished at the way we don't absorb some things when our attention is focused elsewhere. This was illustrated to me by an experiment involving some students, a basketball game and a gorilla . . .

A DAY IN THE LAB

In 1999 a couple of humorous psychologists, Daniel Simons and Christopher Chabris, decided to put the power of single-minded attention to the test. They filmed five minutes of a student basketball game, with one addition. A large man in a gorilla suit was to walk across the court. The film would then be shown to an audience of students to find out what they saw. The basketball players and film crew thought this experiment by Simons and Chabris was mad; surely no one could miss the animal in their midst?

A few days after the shoot, Simons and Chabris gathered a group of students to see the film, asking them to count the number of passes between the team in the white shirts and ignore the men in the black shirts. So what happened? The majority did *not* notice the large gorilla wandering through the match. So Simons and Chabris ran it by them again. Again they didn't notice! What was going on?

Humans are brilliant at focusing their attention – in this case on the ball and the white shirts. The dark-brown gorilla may have been 'seen' by the eyes but was immediately dismissed, demonstrating the unconscious power exerted by our short-term memory to discard everything that our mind deems unhelpful to the task at hand.

Short-term memory performs another vital function, this time to maximize use of the seven 'bits' of knowledge the brain can retain at any one time by rapidly paraphrasing or 'chunking' information, reducing a large amount of complex information to its bare essentials.

Learning how to get to the kernel of a message, and get it through into long-term memory before it disappears, is absolutely vital. Fortunately, parents have an intuitive sense of how fast children can take things in and adjust their speech accordingly.

In many children this ability to paraphrase instructions or explanations develops fast, but for a few, there are difficulties.

ZAC'S STORY

Zac was a friend of my son who sometimes came round to our house after school. At four years old he was a kind, easygoing boy with a great sense of humour and an elephantine memory for facts, but he was often forgetful and constantly in trouble at pre-school. Initially, this was a mystery. In our house, he was always ready to help, but at school he was left dazed in the middle of the classroom while everyone around him went off to do things. It was depressing for Zac and mystified his parents. Time passed, and a reason for his problem eventually emerged when a psychologist discovered that his capacity for short-term memory was alarmingly small. Although he heard what was said, making sense of it was difficult because before the sentence had finished its beginning had disappeared. He had a desperate need to paraphrase but, with everything going too fast, he didn't get enough practice. Zac needed to be spoken to slowly and succinctly, and to be asked to repeat the message back so everyone knew he had grasped it. And that's what happened. But why had it taken so long to find out he had a problem? The answer was that he had developed a phenomenally accurate visual memory and used it to shore up his understanding when long sentences proved difficult. Zac's story is remarkable, not least because he had a brain so flexible he found a way to learn in spite of his problem with memory.

'Chunking' information as it comes into short-term memory requires information – for instance, about the meaning of words and phrases – from long-term memory. To this end, your child will develop a second crucial memory system called 'active working memory'. Active working memory is a vital extension of short-term memory, essential for thinking and reasoning, as well as for deciding how to code and discard incoming information.

Active Working Memory

Human beings think intensively and creatively from dawn to dusk – we just can't stop ourselves. This process is utterly reliant on our being able to gather together a number of thoughts and make something original out of them. That's where active working memory comes in.

Active working memory is a vital space in our mind allowing conscious mental activity. It includes networks that enable us to try out ideas and talk to ourselves, and it can pull out knowledge we already have and bring in things that we are sensing so we can juggle with all sorts of thoughts at once. Active working memory, in fact, enables us to think and it works more efficiently for some people than others. Your child is reliant on his working memory too and you can guess how good it is by looking at how he deals with complicated stories. Children who can put together stories and make inferences from them usually have a good active working memory, while those who get muddled easily may need more practice.

Working memory is necessary for simple tasks too, like knowing what we are going to say before we start to speak, adding a column of figures without losing our place, or deciding what food to cook for dinner; both reasoning and IQ depend on its high performance. Working memory is like a computer's RAM (random access memory), and you can't do anything that requires concentrated, joined-up thinking without it.

Fascinating facts about multi-tasking

Multi-tasking is a modern phenomenon that stretches working memory to its limits. Nowadays we all seem to juggle using the mobile phone, surfing the internet and watching TV while cooking dinner and talking to the kids, thinking that we are getting twice as much done in half the time. But although multi-tasking uses working memory well, it has disadvantages:

- When multi-tasking, we do each task more slowly, often at half the pace, because it takes time to shift our focus from one thing to another. Since we only have one active working memory, when we switch tasks we have to dump our carefully chosen thoughts and drag in new ones, and when we go back to the first task we have probably forgotten where we were and have to start all over again. And let's not forget, once your attention shifts it's irritatingly easy to be distracted by yet another task.
- Because our attention is never totally focused, we tend to make a lot of mistakes, many of which we don't even notice. Lack of time means we rarely achieve intense concentration or 'flow' and so the outcome is not only skimpy, it is also less enjoyable.
- We don't learn much. A psychiatrist has discovered that multi-tasking drives learning away from the part of the brain which processes rich, conscious memories, to an evolutionarily older part called the basal ganglia that is really designed to record simple, automatic activities, and this makes the quality of new learning plummet.
- It is commonly believed that men are not as good at multi-tasking as women, and indeed, women do seem to use more areas of their brain for complex tasks, which might well tip the balance. And, of course, practice makes perfect, so as women tend to juggle more roles than men, they might be expected to multi-task better.

Even the most efficient working memory has its limits, which is why we have to write plans for longer or more complex tasks. One oddity is that it is much easier to do two different tasks – for instance, one verbal and one visual – than to do two similar ones, like 'seeing' two visualizations, at once. This is worth thinking about!

DO IT YOURSELF
Read this sentence once:

A child in his school is not in the garden.

Now shut your eyes and go through the sentence in your mind, saying whether each word is either a noun or a non-noun.

How easy was it? Did you have to concentrate hard? How long did it take you? Did you do it by visualizing the sentence rather than saying it?

Now look at the sentence again, but this time point to nouns and non-nouns.

How easy was that? How long did it take you?

For most of us, pointing is faster and easier. The reason? The verbal part of working memory can only hold one task at a time, so you have to switch between thinking of the test sentence and working out if each word is a noun, whereas when you are pointing at the words the verbal and the visual can be done in tandem.

WHAT YOU CAN DO ... for all children
The things we pay attention to, we learn, so:
- Seize his attention by crouching down to his level and making eye contact.
- Speak or show him slowly and emphatically.
- Ask your child to repeat back what you want him to learn.
- For instance, you could ask him to 'Put your spoon on the plate, it doesn't belong on the floor', then say, 'Now it's your turn, what do you do with the spoon?'

Versions of this technique can be used with children at any age, and, indeed, even with adults if there is something complex that needs to be understood.

WHAT YOU CAN DO ... for babies

- The most important thing you can do for a baby is allow him to focus his attention on whatever pleases him. He will naturally learn by association, imitation and exploration, but he needs to be given plenty of time because he has a lot to learn about even the simplest things.
- Bombarded by sights and sounds, your baby may find it hard to work out what to concentrate on, so try taking him to a quiet room where extraneous noises like cars or other people's conversations cannot be heard.
- Over-stimulated babies get restless and tired and under-stimulated babies get bored, so you will know when you've got it right because he'll be happily and productively engaged.

WHAT YOU CAN DO ... for toddlers and older children

- It is also important for toddlers and older children to learn what to pay attention to. By the time your child is three he will be able to recognize important cues in many situations, but he's still learning, and if he seems muddled it may be that he is not paying attention to the right things. For instance, he won't necessarily hear you talking if he is watching TV.
- By the time your child is five he should be able to paraphrase, reducing a complex instruction to something memorable. I remember the confusion my children felt when they first received instructions like this from a teacher: 'I want you to look at your reading book, and then tomorrow I'll write a list of words on the board and I'll ask each of you to read some of them out to me to make sure you've learnt them. Can you do that? You may need your mother or father to help you.' They were much happier when they learned to paraphrase 'Learn book with Mum, test.'
- Visualizing messages is another useful trick, as most children find pictures easier to understand and more memorable than language.
- There are two simple things you can do to check your child's ability to paraphrase: ask him to tell you what he has understood, and model the task by paraphrasing your own sentences. We used to have a game in our family that involved taking turns to make up a sentence, tailored to each child's level, and getting them to encapsulate it in a few words or pictures. It became a favourite car game, and was frequently very entertaining! For instance, 'We're going to the seaside and we've got our bathers, our sun lotion and buckets and spades and we're going to have an ice-cream.' One of my children paraphrased this as 'Swim. Aaargh sunburn! Mmm ice-cream!' which I thought was great!

- When a list can't be paraphrased it needs to be 'chunked' – that is, put into a memorable format, like PHD ICT (rather than PIDCHT) – if it's to get through short-term memory. Don't forget that even older children can get so lost in complex sentences their working memory gets gridlocked. So have a go, experiment with 'chunking' lists with your child, using pictures as well as words, and adhering to the rule of three and the technique of grouping (see below).
- Maximize your child's power of reasoning by giving his working memory a work-out. Play strategic games that require quick decisions: board games, card games, brain-teasers, quizzes, and simple games like Snap which help develop speed and accuracy.
- Finally, you may notice that your child's working memory doesn't work so well when he is worried. Talking should help, even if peace of mind is not immediately attainable. Leaving him to struggle with a brain full of squirrelling anxiety will make it worse, especially if he feels unappreciated and sad.

A fascinating fact about 'chunking'

We can remember phone numbers only when they are divided into sections of three, four or five digits. For instance, 07575893601 is hard to remember, while 07 575 893 601 is easier. Sets of threes are the easiest groups to remember, and the first five digits of a mobile-phone number can be 'chunked' into 07 – which is the beginning of all mobile numbers – and another three. When 'chunking', it helps if your child knows that groups of threes work well and that putting similar things together can reduce the load further.

Short-term memory and active working memory represent the conscious side of remembering, but we have an ocean of knowledge in
our brain, never seen in its entirety but called upon when needed. It's
called long-term memory and it works in its own idiosyncratic way
– but there are plenty of methods to make it more effective, as you
will see in the next chapter.

The Question of Storage

The mystery of how one and a half kilos of grey matter made largely of fat can handle more information than anything else in the known universe is never likely to be resolved. All we know is that memory works, brilliantly.

Long-term memory seems to be made up of vast networks of brain cells which hold chunks of information to support thinking. But though our brain appears not to be big enough to understand itself, we do know that long-term memory is massive, storing more images, sounds, smells, actions and thoughts than we can imagine, for ever.

A fascinating fact about long-term memory

During World War I, for the first time shrapnel became a major cause of brain damage. Tragic as this was for the men concerned, neuroscience benefited, for when the wounded soldiers were tested, brain surgeons and neurologists started to unlock the secrets of the mind.

Scientists had long wanted to know where long-term memories reside, but what they discovered in this flurry of research was surprising. Memory is everywhere, dispersed over the massive network of nerves and grey matter that make up the brain. Memory loss, they found, was related more to the volume of brain that was damaged than to any one place. This meant that if there was brain damage in one area, the wounded soldiers could often learn to find memories by another route. That's one reason why old memories are especially robust – we've got lots of ways to get at them.

Long-term memories seem to form gradually by tiny but permanent changes to the brain. There are several different processes. 'Procedural memory' is formed when we learn to do an activity and is then used without conscious thought. For instance, we don't have to recall how to take every step, we just walk – and the chances are we don't even remember learning how to do it. There are thousands of these automatic skills, ranging from knowing which way to turn a screwdriver to riding a bike. These basic memories get into our brain through parts that are ancient in evolutionary terms, where the subconscious rules.

How unlike that is our conscious memory, and how we struggle to grasp what we know is there. Memories are slippery things. Some are factual, some halfway to fiction, some photographically vivid, others a fuzzy mixture of thoughts and emotions. And everyone has a reservoir of forgotten memories lurking in the brain, which surface occasionally in dreams or when triggered by a reminiscent smell or sound. These memories are not placed whole into the brain; they go in little by little through an extraordinary organ called the hippocampus, the Greek name for a sea horse, which it oddly resembles. I spent three years investigating this part of the brain; it is one of the common foci for epilepsy, not surprisingly because, unusually, its nerves feed back positively on themselves so the electrical activity can spiral out of control. But the feedback is necessary for the laying-down of memories, continuously linking out to the rest of the brain and gradually, over months, spreading a spider's web of information, a shadowy simulacrum of an event carved out in tiny changes through hundreds of brain cells.

Terrible things happen if this mechanism doesn't work, as I discovered when we met with an intelligent young man called Jon.

JON'S STORY

Twenty-six-year-old Jon Forbes can't remember what happened yesterday. His past and his future are a blank. His bedroom is covered in Post-it notes, reminders of things done and things he wants to do, which he reads and immediately forgets. Yet Jon is a keen quiz master, hosting competitions in the drop-in centre where he works. So what has happened to his memory? And why? The answer lies deep in his brain.

Jon was nine and had four years of schooling under his belt before his tragic condition was discovered. Jon's mother Beverley remembers the day with crystal clarity.

'Jon and I went shopping. As we came down the high street there was an Indian lady wearing a golden sari with a python round her neck. Jon was really excited. He rushed up to her and no one else got a look-in because he was chatting so much! He was so happy. So when we got home I asked Jon to tell his father all about it and Jon said, "All about what, Mum? " and I said, "You know, about the lady you talked to ... the Indian lady ... the snake?" Jon looked at me completely blankly and everything seemed to go silent. Lots of things fell into place. And that was when we knew.'

Beverley took Jon to a specialist, where the reason for his situation was revealed. His hippocampus, the part of the brain that lays memories down, was only 3cm long, less than half yours or mine. The hippocampus is especially vulnerable to a lack of oxygen around birth and Jon was born very prematurely, in a hospital that didn't have enough ventilators. Jon's twin sister, Jane, in an even worse state, was raced to be ventilated in another hospital, where she died, but Jon was kept alive by nurses who sat with him twenty-four hours a day, flicking his feet whenever he stopped breathing.

From his birth as a premature baby to his ninth year, Jon covered up his memory gap by rote learning, repeating information over and over, stamping it into his mind. But his absence of memory, once discovered, was not treatable and Jon faces a life where his mind is void of everyday human experience. He keeps a diary to remind him of plans for the immediate future, but happy moments and tragic ones are lost in an instant, along with any knowledge of where he has been, who he has seen and what he has done.

It seems like a life half lived, but Jon is not unhappy. He's got a sense of humour, a job he loves and is adept at concealing his disability, going out on the town with his long-term friend, Steve, who shares his love of bowling and science fiction. There is also a seemingly miraculous exception to his amnesia.

Strong emotion can make strong memories, bypassing the usual mechanisms. Jon now has a girlfriend and, amazingly, can still remember their first date. The lesson? Never underestimate the power of love!

Repetition and frequent recall, salience, novelty, context and, especially, emotion all help to strengthen memories, but all memories have to be retrievable, and that means they need to be filed in the right places, linked to useful reminders. This process starts early: children work up from remembering the rules that define objects and allow recognition (a dog always has four legs, a furry coat and a black nose) to remembering the rules that define groups of objects (things in the bedroom, family, animals), to remembering the rules that define the customary way we do things. These last are called schemas and are really just stories about habitual behaviours which we use as templates on which to hang atypical events. Young children who are still learning the schema itself can be unsettled if their understanding of a situation is not respected.

Kerri speaks

Ethan knows what happens in supermarkets because his mother, Kerri, used to work in one and in his schema, closing hours loom large.

> *When we go to the supermarket and he hears "The shop will be closing in the next half-hour" Ethan will literally grab the trolley and say, "Come on, Mummy, come on, come on, come on," and I'm like, "No Ethan, no, they're not closing yet," but Ethan really worries. "But they're closing, they're closing and we'll be locked in here all night!" he says. I try to see the world through his eyes; it's a horrible, bad world out there and if I can keep it as nice and fun as possible, I will. But he's got a very active imagination. Sometimes that's good, but sometimes not.*

Ethan's supermarket story tells him he must get out well before closing time, otherwise he'll be locked in, alone, scared and in the dark for the night. So it's not surprising that he's very unsettled by his mother's lack of urgency.

WHAT YOU CAN DO ... for babies

- None of us remembers much before the age of two; even so, your baby's long-term memory is developing. She learns to recognize people and places and uses her body to learn procedures. Encourage experimentation, point out interesting differences (to a baby, a bird and an aeroplane seem to be pretty much the same thing!) and remember that she is setting down a filing system that in two years' time will facilitate conscious recall.

WHAT YOU CAN DO ... for toddlers and older children

- One of the wonderful things your child's brain will do is make filing systems, schemas and stories that are totally adapted to her needs. Offering her lots of different categories to play with, like finding things that are blue or describing a typical day with her grandma will give her a rich tapestry in which to place her memories. Then her imagination and memory will work together to cement those schemas and stories that act as short-cuts, giving a context

around which individual exceptions can be filed.

- Building a memory for past events can be huge fun. As soon as your child can talk, let her tell you about what's going on in her life. She is unlikely to give you a blow-by-blow account because children usually don't (see p.194 for talking tips), but she will remember the best and worst of her day and talking will keep her event memory in top condition. She will keep the memories fresh if you remind her of what happened a month ago or this time last year. You can even keep a diary together, using pictures. She'll love having clear memories – and an aide-memoire – when she's older.

- As she gets older go on encouraging knowledge-building, but now you can talk about how to categorize things – animals and plants, machines and natural objects, even types of car. Small children are hungry for knowledge but their filing systems are rudimentary, though they can build up fast. For instance, the first time your child sees a dog she will have to set up a new file and put everything about this strange creature in it, but when she encounters another dog, she'll only need to file its individual characteristics, which is much faster. The more experience she has, the faster her memory's filing system will grow and the easier it will become to remember new things.

A fascinating fact about left-handed people

Oddly, left-handed people often recall events better than right-handers. Scans of the brain show that, while right-handed people have their language centres fixed in the left half of the brain and some visual, creative elements concentrated in the right, left-handed people have less specialization and more connections between the right and left as a result. This aids memory because more links are made between one bit of memory and another.

But there is more to long-term memory than creating good filing systems. Over the years people have discovered powerful ways to increase memory, by using rhymes and sentences, emotions and our senses, especially our powerful sense of direction. The people who use these well are extraordinary. I've been talking to some of them and know that their stories will help your children learn the ancient art of memorizing by heart.

Memory Tricks

Your child will face up to a hundred exams before he leaves school. These exams are important – the passport to a good job and financial security. To pass them, he will have to memorize thousands of facts, figures and theories. Knowing how to remember them is absolutely crucial.

Exciting events are easy for your child to remember in comparison with facts which can lack emotional and personal impact. A talent for memorizing facts needs to be developed early and exercised for ever. Use it, test it, ask questions, and if you still have difficulties you can adopt tricks called 'mnemonics' – an unpronounceable and hopelessly forgettable word – used by the greatest practitioners in the world. Your child can benefit from the technique, because mnemonics work.

Memorizing Lists and Facts by Using Rhymes, First Letters and Games

DO IT YOURSELF

We all know a few rhymes or sentences that help with memorizing lists and facts. These are the ones I was brought up with:

A bit of spelling:

> *I before E except after C.*

A bit of astronomy:

> *My Very Eager Mother Just Served Us Nine Pizzas*
> (Mercury, Venus, Earth, Mars, Jupiter, Saturn,
> Uranus, Neptune, Pluto – in order, from the sun out.)

A bit of science:

> *Richard Of York Gave Battle In Vain*
> (Red, Orange, Yellow, Green, Blue, Indigo and
> Violet – the colours of the rainbow in order.)

A bit of history:

> *In fourteen hundred and ninety-two*
> *Columbus sailed the ocean blue.*

A bit of music:

> *Every Good Boy Deserves Favour*
> (The notes on the lines of a treble clef,
> starting at the bottom.)

And a bit of everyday knowledge:

> *Thirty days hath September, April, June and November.*
> *All the rest have thirty-one, excepting February alone,*
> *Which has twenty-eight days clear,*
> *And twenty-nine in each leap year.*

My mother taught me a different way to remember the number of days in the month: knuckle counting, which your child will find easier. Don't be put off by how long it takes to explain – it really is simple!

Clench your fists and count the months off on the knuckles and the hollows between them, moving from left to right. Months that fall on the knuckle have 31 days: January – the knuckle on the far left – has 31 days, February – in the hollow – has 28 or 29, March – on the next knuckle – has 31, April – in the next hollow – has 30, and so on. July (31 days) falls on the fourth knuckle of your left hand, and August (31 days again) on the first knuckle of your right hand. Keep going until you get to December. Simple!

As I was writing this book, I came across the origins of this method. Southern Europeans, spreading East to China and West to South America, use knuckle counting, whereas Northern people use variants of the rhyme above.

Try some of these mnemonics with your child, and make up new ones tailored to his age and interests. It will be easy to fix the sentence, rhyme or song in your child's mind – the trick is to attach it to the meaning, and you can only do that by practising. Unless, of course, you manage to invent one that contains a reminder of the subject!

Mnemonics can also help us remember lists of numbers. Telephone numbers, as we have established, are more easily remembered by grouping them in chunks of three or four, or, if you prefer, by visualizing the pattern they make on the phone. Drawing diagrams to organize and link facts is another useful memory aid, as many of our children are better at 'seeing' with their mind's eye than remembering words.

Memorizing Using Visualization and Journeys

Your child's brain is much more active than yours and it needs to be, because until he has got a really effective filing system, he will go on using all his senses and brain power to work out what should be remembered. As he learns, his memory will improve and he will soon surprise you with the accuracy of his recall, especially when given precise cues – and there is no known limit to memory growth. However, there are some tasks that children do better than adults, because adults have forgotten something important.

DO IT YOURSELF

Try reading these words:

man, pat, hat, lap, bat.

Now turn away and remember them. How many do you remember?

Now read these words:

pit, date, cow, peg, sun.

How many do you remember this time?

What about your child? Read the first list out, and see what he remembers. Now try the second.

Now try to repeat the two lists once more. Has one stuck in your mind better than the other?

Most people don't get the first set of simple words right. The difficulty comes because the words sound similar. P and B, for instance, are particularly muddling. You probably remembered more of the second list, because they sound more distinctive. But children usually remember the first list better because, instead of remembering the word itself, they visualize its meaning.

Try doing what children do: visualize the object rather than repeating the word. You will probably find it easier to remember, which just goes to show that using more than one sense helps us to learn.

The human brain is designed to latch on to stories, especially if they are visualized, partly because they generally follow a predictable and logical trajectory, with a beginning – introducing character and plot – an action-packed middle and a satisfying denouement. Jokes are short stories with clever endings; lectures are long ones, with predictable endings; but both are more memorable than unconnected facts. So what should we do when we have to remember an incomprehensible list of facts? There is an answer …

BEN'S STORY

Inside the examination halls at Oxford University, the ability to tell an elaborate story using unconnected characters and objects, then to remember it, was being pushed to the absolute limit. We were witnessing the annual World Memory Championship with Ben Pridmore, who knows the secret of success.

Ben says: 'I suppose you could call me some kind of storyteller. It's a very restricted kind of story, though. I only have 2,704 different characters to feature in it and quite a lot of those are inanimate objects so it doesn't get all that thrilling.'

Ben associates his images with things he wants to remember. It's this technique that has made him the world record-holder for memorizing the impossibly huge strings of binary numbers. He can memorize a random sequence of three thousand digits in less than an hour.

Ben makes it sound easy: 'Remembering three thousand ones and zeros isn't as complicated as it might sound, because each group of ten I convert into a mental picture like, say, a pack of cards, or a rubber duck or a lamp, and I place each picture along a route, say, from here to Oxford railway station, and see them in my head. So it's really just remembering three hundred pretty pictures, and a lot easier to remember than a lot of straight ones and zeros.'

Ben associates his random list of zeros and ones with pictures and he places each picture in a place on a known route, making memorable incongruous visualizations. Try it! You and I may not be as good as Ben, but everyone can make this technique work for smaller lists.

Ben has no doubt about the brain's capacity. He says: 'Everybody has the potential to use their brain to a much greater extent than they actually do, and when it comes to memory, nobody has even scratched the surface of what is possible!'

Making up stories, rhymes and songs, using all our senses, visualizing a journey and placing incongruous and memorable objects along the route – these techniques can be used alone or in combination. And there are other things you can do.

WHAT YOU CAN DO ... for all children

- The more your child learns, the more he will be able to learn. The space in his brain won't run out – quite the reverse, it will just get bigger and more effective. In London the drivers of black cabs are licensed only when they have got 'the Knowledge' – the names and positions of twenty-five thousand streets. Scientists have discovered that the part of their brain that deals with mapping and spatial awareness actually grows bigger during this time. In just the same way, different areas of your brain will benefit from your types of learning. The message is use it or lose it!

A fascinating fact about gender and navigation

Women and men tend to learn how to map-read using different cues. Women tend to use landmarks more often and men think more spatially, using diagrams. But the brains of both men and women are designed to do both – and because knowing routes was so important during our early evolution, there is a particular part of the brain that takes special notice of landmarks when we change direction. These landmarks are placed in our unconscious, to be recalled when we use that route again.

WHAT YOU CAN DO ... for toddlers

- It's well known that many two-year-olds spend too much time lolling in front of the TV – some for as many as six hours a day. But some television programmes can be good aids to learning, providing stories, sights, songs and conversation to stimulate emotions, and repetition, all potent aids to memory. So watching appropriate programmes with your toddler and rehearsing the lessons with him will pay dividends.

WHAT YOU CAN DO ... for older children

- Encourage your older child to make up mnemonics, especially funny ones, and put them to music!
- Four-year-olds already have a good memory and you can help by continuing to encourage your child to use his senses. For instance, if you want him to remember to take a snack to school, ask him to picture himself walking out of your home and into the classroom with his snack box in his hand. Your child will also be able to help himself learn to read by visualizing and reciting letters, or to learn to play the recorder by remembering precisely how it feels to hold the instrument and place his fingers.
- Take a lead from memory man, Ben Pridmore, and encourage your child to remember streams of facts by using his navigation and story-telling skills. It is easier to master this skill when young, and once he has done so, he will be able to use it for ever.

Forgetting the Real and Remembering the False

'I have a memory like an elephant. In fact, elephants often consult me.' Noel Coward

According to myth, the elephant has one great trick – it never forgets, unlike you, me and Noel Coward. Coward knew that the absurdity of his joke would also make people laugh for another reason: because none of us has exactly the same memories as anyone else. Memory is enigmatic and unreservedly personal. And while some people claim that we remember all our experiences, we are actually adept at for-getting – a good thing, because every second of every day we are bombarded with images, sounds and feelings that together make up a staggering amount of information. While short-term memory ac-tively rejects everything not salient or relevant, long-term memories can silently fade away until only the important elements remain.

There are many things we forget and never miss. But memory can be capricious. There are things we wish to forget but can't, memories we know are there but can't find, and even events we remember – although they never happened.

Misplaced Memories

It is tantalizingly easy to forget things. Recalling facts, names and even events is harder than recognizing them, and reminders don't always help. Think about how many people you've met for the ump-teenth time and still can't remember their name! 'Tip of the tongue' syndrome is common for children as well as adults, and happens because the words they are looking for have not been sufficiently well attached to a reminder. One strategy that can work is to give the person/place/word a character. For instance, remembering a name that has no association other than a face can be easier if you add an adjective like 'Spotty Sam' or 'Bald Barry'. Emotion not only has a profound impact on what types of things we can recall, it also changes what we forget, as a test we did on some *Child of Our Time* parents shows.

A fascinating fact about emotions and forgetting

We decided to ask fifty adults to recall five happy memories, followed by five unhappy memories, as fast as they could. The results were striking. About half of them told us they had forgotten most of their unhappy memories, while readily recalling lots of happy times. The other half of our group did the opposite: they were able to remember with painful clarity their unhappiness but struggled to recall what had made them happy. Why is this? The answer is that our brain gives us easy access to memories that align with the mood we are in, and struggles to find memories coloured by a different mood.

To get round this you need to actively change your mood, which can be done with music or by absorbing yourself in good (or bad) memories – if you can think of any! – until your mood has shifted. By the same token, making yourself feel happy gives you access to your best moments and increases happiness, while wallowing in misery will only make life seem worse.

Associations between situation and mood are especially powerful for children, whose reliance on language and words is less sophisticated than yours.

Intrusive Memories

Emotion can also bring out intrusive memories, things we would like to forget, but can't. The capacity to remember disasters is clearly important for survival: we need our children to remember that cars can run people over and that eating poisonous substances is a bad idea. But we also remember embarrassing moments, tragedy and trauma, and these can haunt us for ever and may colour our lives. So the ability to suppress intrusive memories is a vital life skill and worth practising when you are very young. Introducing happy memories or working through unhappy ones until they become devoid of emotion are both useful tactics. Interestingly, forgetting the bad and remembering the good is linked positively with creativity, in that creative people seem by nature more able to forget disaster. More negatively, anxiety conversely reduces the impetus to be creative.

False Memories

Surprisingly, the mind is perfectly capable of inventing memories that are indistinguishable from the real thing. This happens for several reasons. We may mix two or three different memories, we may see something interesting and associate it with ourselves, or we may simply imagine something. But the most potent of our false memories happen when we witness something that doesn't make sense. Many of us subconsciously reframe, and the new interpretation is remembered as both truthful and accurate. This 'evidence' is very potent for children, whose memory is less certain than adults' – but even adults can succumb to false memory, as we showed in a day in the lab.

A DAY IN THE LAB

We showed a group of adults photographs from their childhood, garnered from grandparents who were in on the secret. We took one of the photos and tampered with it so it seemed to be evidence that they had, as a child, gone up in a hot-air balloon, although, in fact, none of them had ever done such a trip. When they were first shown the photo they were all surprised and, of course, none of them remembered the event. But two weeks later, after giving the matter some thought, three out of the six tested were convinced the balloon ride had happened and had even constructed some vivid memories of it. This is what one said:

Caroline: 'I was fairly aghast when I saw the picture first, thinking "Aargh! I really have been up in a hot-air balloon!" … but thinking back over the past fortnight it slowly came back to me and I do remember. It was a summer fete and we didn't actually go right up into the sky, as it was attached by a rope.'

In a much larger study, half the participants recalled some memory of the hot-air balloon; they were all enviably strong on creativity and visualization.

It turns out that many imaginative adults fall for this trick. Perhaps it's not surprising, because the very same brain cell networks that hold memories of real events also process ideas, so real memories, thoughts, logic and imagination can get mixed up, as they must if we are to engage in joined-up thinking. But this necessary and seemingly innocent process can sometimes cause a great deal of trouble.

JAKE AND LINCOLN'S STORY

Jake and Lincoln are actors who took part in an experiment which a psychologist friend carried out some years ago to find out about the accuracy of eye-witness testimony. The experiment took place on a crowded train. Jake, who is white, and Lincoln, who is black, got into the carriage talking amicably, but after a few minutes staged a violent disagreement. Jake pulled out a knife and made to injure Lincoln. Just at this moment the train doors opened and Lincoln and Jake ran for it.

Afterwards, the psychologist asked the passengers to describe the scene. Most of the witnesses swore that Lincoln had carried the knife and that Jake was the victim – exactly the opposite of what had really happened. They were so certain they would have sworn it in court. But all it proved is that the witnesses themselves were unconsciously racist. They 'knew' the black man must be guilty because otherwise it didn't make sense, and so they subconsciously transferred the knife to Lincoln's hand. This disturbing experiment has been used to counter accusations from eye-witnesses in court cases, and it teaches us an important lesson about memory and the power of belief over rationality.

WHAT YOU CAN DO ... for all children

- There are some things we cannot forget: they are written into our very being. Even the tiniest baby knows her mother when she hears her voice. Older children look at a switch and know it will turn on a light; still older ones attach names to faces and words to their meaning. Helping your child remember these associations will help her navigate her world safely.
- Emotions are particularly powerful in creating memories, both pleasant and unpleasant. Bad experiences can colour her mood for a long time, but you can help by minimizing their importance, or by re-interpreting them so they become neutral, or even positive. Encouraging your child to build a positive picture of her life will help her remember the good things and make her happy!

WHAT YOU CAN DO ... for toddlers

- Misplaced memories can be found with a cue, and then rehearsed so they won't be forgotten again. It is especially useful to add a tag. Barmy Brian will make you smile and be hard to forget!
- Toddlers are particularly prone to scary memories, so watch out for these and be proactive in defusing them. And toddlers have great imaginations, so the proof that there is no monster in her room at night has to be convincing. You may know what your child is scared of, but you may need to be imaginative to banish her fear!

WHAT YOU CAN DO ... for older children

- Your older child can use more sophisticated cues for recall. Encourage her to fish for the desired information by coming up with a first letter or a visualization of a place, picture or person. The more often your child is able to find the memory herself the better, making well-worn routes to her own knowledge.
- False memories come into play more with older children, and aren't necessarily damaging. However, children are very sensitive to cultural norms, which they absorb without you knowing, from assumptions about ethnicity to negative views of fat people. These can give rise to damaging false memories, so it is worthwhile challenging them. That way you'll not only find out if your child is making erroneous deductions, you will also help her to think for herself.

Memory is quite amazing. Only seven items can fit into short-term memory at any one time, yet we can process them so fast we are unaware of any glitches. New long-term memories will be established if they are important, contextualized and emotionally laden, which means that if you want or need to learn something, you probably will. But learning is one thing, recall is another, and the key to that is rehearsal. If you think about something many times it will never fade away. Active memory is where we do our thinking, relying on stored memories and input into short-term memory. And yet memory still plays tricks on us, the most notable being our capacity to brew up false memories. Maybe I have one of my own …

JUDITH'S STORY

Some years ago, my sister Judith and I discovered a walk in Wales which we had done when we were young. We must have been about ten and eight at the time, and we both re-membered it. It was long and arduous on the way up, but on the way down my father found a scree – a few hundred yards of loose slate on the flank of the mountain. Jump on a scree and you can find yourself sliding rapidly down the mountain-side and, in this case, come perilously close to a cold lake in the valley below.

Judith and I have different views on mountain climbing. She loves going up, strong and steady, trudging to the sum-mit. I prefer coming down in a series of loping strides, con-trolled falling that is almost without effort. So we arrived at the scree with very different ambitions. I wanted to slide, Judith preferred the path. Unable to compromise, we sat in the sunshine and ate our sandwiches, looking over the scree and wondering what decision my father had reached all those years ago. It was the cold lake and the recollection of deep disappointment that made me sure our father had not taken us down the scree, but Judith, remembering fear and bruises, was certain he had.

So there we were, my sister and I, sitting on a deserted mountain, arguing fiercely. Only when the last crumb was eaten and the sun past its zenith did we realize there was no one left alive to tell us the truth. We laughed ruefully at that and finished the walk on the path, reminiscing happily all the way back to the car.

It is our personal remembrances that make us who we are, and if memory is an occasionally faulty storehouse for learning, thinking is its zenith. Thinking is something we humans do brilliantly, using reason to understand our world and strategy to plan it. In the next section I will show you how language, maths, creativity, music and art underpin thinking. But in the first section, find out how astonishingly quickly your child becomes the ultimate logician.

PART FOUR:
THINK!

There's one fault that I find with the twentieth century
And I'll put it in a couple of words: too adventurey.
What I'd like is some nice dull monotony
If anyone's gotony.

Ogden Nash

In our 'adventurey' world where there always seems too much to do and not enough time to do it, a little bit of monotony is just what we need. Ruminating quietly may seem a shocking waste of time, but it is only then that ideas bubble to the surface, enthusing us and our families and even changing the world …

CHILDREN OF THE CARIBBEAN'S STORY

Eighteen years ago in the Caribbean island of Jamaica, a young researcher called Sally McGregor started an inspirational project. She had found out that a large number of impoverished six-year-olds were arriving at school virtually unable to learn. Whatever the teacher did and however long they stayed at school, they didn't make much progress.

McGregor wanted to know why, so she visited the most disadvantaged suburbs and found many malnourished and neglected babies. Their delayed development could have been put down to the dearth of food, but McGregor had an idea that other forces were at work. With a little money at her disposal she set up a careful test. She provided one set of babies with extra milk and cornmeal, and sent a child expert to a second set, who visited once a week for two years to teach mothers how to play with their children. A third set was given both food and social-intellectual stimulation, and the fourth was a comparison group of children who were not disadvantaged.

Two years later, the children were tested for IQ and general development. The group who were not disadvantaged did well, as expected. So what happened to the other three groups? All of them made remarkable progress, with a combination of extra food and play resulting in the most dramatic improvement. But at that crucial point, McGregor's team had to withdraw, leaving their vulnerable two-and-a-half-year-olds in poor conditions.

Fortunately the story doesn't end there. Three years later, when the children started school, McGregor tested them

again. Imagine her surprise when she realized that, though they had not profited much in the long term from having better food, those who had been stimulated intellectually and socially when they were babies were still reaping the benefit and were nearly as intellectually able as any of their classmates.

I was told this story by a Jamaican friend, Dr Maureen Samms-Vaughan. Eighteen years after the project started, the teenagers are still more intelligent than they would have been without early stimulation. This great idea has borne fruit and, due to Samms-Vaughan's enthusiasm, other children today in some of the worst-off families on the island are getting help because she knows that if a young child is able to play and be excited by learning he will be better off for ever.

Researchers from disciplines as far apart as child psychology and management consultancy agree that children's formative early years are crucial to being able to think rationally, creatively and productively as adults. I'm going to show you how thinking skills develop in clear stages, and how your child learns to use the power of words, numbers, art and music.

But there is something we have to accept. Neither cramming nor neglect will help your child learn how to use the amazing tools for thinking that nature has provided. The tremendous changes that take place between the ages of two and seven – social, emotional, intellectual – happen only *because* your child is ruminating, learning, talking and imagining.

Thinking Basics

'Minds are like parachutes; they operate only when open.' Thomas Dewar changed the Victorian industrial landscape with his inventions, helping to make Britain one of the richest countries in the world. If your child opens his mind and ponders the big issues of life, he can change the world too.

The truth is that all humans think intently from dawn to dusk, but unfortunately at least half our thoughts are extremely dull and very, very few are actually innovative! Scientists have shown that most of the time our infinitely capable brain is used to preen ourselves and to worry about minutiae – dinner, clothes and being late. But thinking is more important than that. First, the basics:

Do Objects Exist?

- Newborns examine boundaries because they are trying to distinguish objects from their background. They quickly learn that objects exist.
- At three months, your young baby may accidentally push some thing out of sight. Watch what happens next. He'll look startled, maybe cross, but won't look for it because he doesn't yet know that objects exist when he can't see them. Out of sight is out of mind.
- By the time he is six months old he'll be dropping things for fun and will realize both that they fall and that they don't just disappear, they end up on the floor.
- Nine-month-olds have trouble finding things. They will look for something if they see where it has been hidden, but, with fatal logic, believe that a toy will be found in its last hiding place, not in a new one. Even three-month-old kittens understand more!

DO IT YOURSELF

Show your nine- or ten-month-old baby a toy, hide it within reach and see if he finds it. If he does, hide it somewhere else close at hand while he is watching. He will go to the first hiding place as 'the place where the toy goes when I can't see it'. This bewildering phase lasts for a couple of months.

What Are Tools For?

- Give your child a toy rake and an out-of-reach toy at around eighteen months and he will, for the first time, realize that he can use the rake to get the toy. This attainment marks the beginning of strategic thinking: doing something in order to achieve something else.

Who Am I?

- One-year-olds, like dogs, don't realize that the person they see in the mirror is them, because they can't think about themselves as a person.
- Two-year-olds don't yet realize that other people have minds and feelings that are different from theirs, so they assume that you feel what they feel, which means they really don't understand why snatching toys causes trouble! It takes several years for a child to learn how to see things from someone else's point of view.

What Is Time?

- Three-year-olds have difficulty imagining the passage of time. They know breakfast time is after they wake up and that pre-school ends when it's time to go home, 'yesterday' is a very elastic term and otherwise there is 'now' and 'not now'. You'll know your child has grasped the nature of time when, several years on, he agrees when you say you'll do something in half an hour and doesn't pester you!

Are Things What They Appear?

- Four-year-olds put a misplaced trust in appearances. For them, things that are longer are bigger, and people who are taller are older. This is also true of quantities, as you can see from the game below. There is even a point at which your child believes that if a boy puts on girls' clothes he has become a girl!

The *Child of Our Time* children speak

Our four-year-olds were given Ken and Barbie dolls and asked to tell us what gender they were. Not surprisingly, they all got it right. Then their clothes were swapped …

Young children cross-dress Ken and tell us that he has become a girl!

Researcher:	Is Ken a boy or a girl?
Calvin:	A girl!
Researcher:	What if we cut that doll's hair off?
William:	It will be a boy and if we put back his long hair then it would be a girl.
Eve:	Because men don't wear dresses!

- Four-year-olds often believe that gender is fluid and feel it is safer to stick with the rules rigidly – which is one reason why boys are genuinely scared of wearing pink!
- Five-year-olds are still egocentric enough to find it hard to come to grips with life's less comforting realities, believing that their road is bigger than the rest of the city, and that a small amount of money will be enough to buy a house.

DO IT YOURSELF

Put out a line of ten pennies, well spread out. Then put out another line of ten pennies, closer together. Ask your three- or four-year-old which has the most pennies. Chances are she'll think it's the long line. Try the same trick with water. Pour water from a measuring jug into a tall thin glass and, with her helping, pour exactly the same amount into a short fat glass. Even though she knows the same amount of water went in, she will still think that the tall thin glass has more.

Rules Are Rules. Aren't They?

- Six-year-olds tend to be rigid about facts and rules. It can make them seem blocked and unadventurous, but, in fact, it's an important stage, the basis from which refinements and clarifications can be thought through. An example you can try yourself involves balancing weights on a fulcrum.
- Seven is an important milestone. At seven your child knows himself and is, at last, confident with the physical rules that govern the world.

DO IT YOURSELF

You need a rod, a fulcrum to balance it on, and a weight – anything that you can stick or tie on to the rod will do.

Then ask your child to balance the rod on the fulcrum, first without a weight and then with a small weight attached to one side, heavy enough to unbalance it.

Watch how your child tackles the task of rebalancing.

You should find that a clear pattern emerges. A three-year-old child will experiment until the rod is balanced, whatever weight is on it, and so will a seven- or eight-year-old. But between these ages your child will know that most rods balance in the middle, and when it doesn't he will get frustrated but won't think to try a different spot. He is wrong, of course, but brilliantly logical, using the rule he knows. It will take someone to point out that balance is not really to do with length, but with weight, before he will try out something different.

One of the things you will have noticed from the list above is how immensely hard your child works to find things out, and, en route to seven, you will notice how much his logical conclusions matter to him.

BAZ'S STORY

Baz was three when I drove him and his parents to visit mutual friends. He was a thoughtful boy and for much of the journey silently sucked his thumb and slept. But one sight fascinated him. It was a sugar-beet factory spewing out billows of white vapour from its huge chimneys. His mother responded with a vague 'Lovely! Clouds of steam!' and that seemed to be the end of it. But it wasn't. Many months later, Baz was at pre-school and proudly declared that clouds were made by factories all over the country and were pushed out through really big chimneys. Everyone laughed, except Baz, who knew that his information was entirely logical and was determined to make everyone understand. Back home his mother discussed the mistake with him, but Baz was not satisfied. It seemed to him that his mother's explanation – that clouds are made when warm air from the sea rises over the hills and cools down – didn't fit the evidence he had seen with his own eyes. And Baz not only defended his idea because he believed in his brilliant deductive logic but also as a result of bitter personal experience. Earlier that week his sister had laughed at him for believing in Father Christmas. Baz had frequently been told that things don't materialize from thin air, and was in no mood to believe that was how clouds were made.

It's clear that even young children can use induction and deduction to bolster an argument, and even when they are wrong, they are right!

Your child does have an amazing talent for thinking, but there is one barrier that may mask his ability. He may be brilliant at immersing himself in what he is doing, but find it impossible to switch attention, so if you ask him a question unrelated to what he's doing he's highly likely to look blank and tell you he doesn't know – even if you know he does! He hasn't yet learnt the trick of switching momentarily to answer a question and immediately switching back. In fact, shutting the rest of the world out is a prerequisite for really deep thinking, and it entails something that we do automatically.

DO IT YOURSELF

There are some conditions that make it impossible to think, because they stop you concentrating. Try this and see what happens to you ...

Think about a tricky problem that you have ...

Now say where your eyes were while you were thinking.

You are unlikely to have been looking at the book or at a person. Your gaze probably went up and to the left.

Most right-handed people shift their eyes to the left if presented with a verbal question. Many left-handers look straight up or to the right, depending how their brain is wired.

Try this experiment with your child: Tell him to look at you and then ask questions you are sure he knows the answer to, reminding him to keep his eyes on your face.

Can he still perform?

We did this experiment with five-year-olds from the *Child of Our Time* project. They knew the answers to all the questions, but this is what they did when they had to maintain eye contact with our researcher:

Researcher:	Jamie, a kitten grows up to be a cat. Can you tell me what a lamb grows up to be?
Jamie	*(squirms in his seat, grimaces and finally ...)*: A chick ... a chicken.
Researcher:	What does a lamb grow up to be? Look at my face.
Mabel	*(after some considerable time, very uncertain)*: A big lamb?

None of us can maintain focus when looking at something that grabs us, and it's especially disastrous if we look at other people because we are programmed to watch them carefully, presumably because people are the primary source of love and danger.

One of the important things that children learn early on is that some things are right and some wrong. They discover these rules through thinking and working things out; helped by their carers, their teachers and their own nature. By the time your child is three he will be using rules to master speech. It's at this stage that he will forget that the past tense of 'go' is 'went', and start saying 'goed'. A year later, he will have refined his language rules and acknowledge irregularities. 'Goed' quickly moves back to 'went'. But the process goes on as children get older and complex moral rules crop up. These, too, are first felt to be binding, then modified as new more sophisticated rules take their place. But during this process, children may get cross when things are not done the 'right' way. A rule, they feel, is a rule.

DO IT YOURSELF

Young children think rules cannot be broken, as this little test demonstrates. I have labelled the child in the story as a boy, but if your own child is a girl, call the child in the dilemma a girl too, as that will help your daughter identify with the issue. This is the story you are to tell:

'A little boy's mother is very ill and about to die. The chemist in his town has some special medicine that would cure her but it is too expensive for the family to buy. His father tries hard to borrow the money, but he can only manage to raise half of it. So he goes to the chemist and asks him to sell it cheaply, but the chemist refuses because he wants to make money out of it. So the father gets desperate and breaks into the shop to steal the medicine for his wife. Should the husband have done that?'

Few children under about seven think it is right to steal, even for so important a reason. But at around nine, children start to understand hierarchies of need, and realize that, in some instances, stealing might be more important than abiding by the rules.

I have told many children this tale: here are three thoughtful responses from children on the cusp of understanding the ambivalence of the 'don't steal' rule.

Maisie's View (Aged Seven)
'It was a bad thing, but no, he should have bought it and he could have given the money he had to the chemist.'

Katy's View (Aged Eight and a Half)
(After a long think.) 'I think yes *and* no. It's nice for him to make that effort to save his wife. No because he shouldn't have stolen the medicine, but I wouldn't send him to prison because he should be there for his wife.'

Anna's View (Also Aged Eight and a Half)

'Well … I'm not really sure. It's sort of yes because … no … wait … no. I don't think he should have stolen it, because he could have done something good for the chemist instead. He could just have let her die because it's better not to be in pain. He can't just steal the medicine because they'll track him down. Though I suppose he could steal the medicine and then move to another town.'

It takes a long time to learn when to break rules and en route your young child will indulge in a lot of egocentric wishful thinking, on the assumption that he miraculously causes everything to happen and that other people's thoughts are exactly the same as his. It is not surprising, then, that toddlers can be jubilant when other people are happy and may get very upset when someone breaks something or if parents argue. But over time, your child will begin to learn to understand other people's minds.

DO IT YOURSELF

This simple game shows how difficult it is for young children to realize that other people have different minds.

Take a coin, hide it in one of your hands and ask your child to guess where it is. He'll try and if he gets it wrong, will laugh and try again.

Ask him to play the same trick on you.

We played this game with the *Child of Our Time* children when they were three and a half and this is what happened: the children either laughed and said 'You know!' and showed their parent the coin, or they just showed them, with a mystified air, clearly wondering what sort of game this was. Only one boy managed to play this properly – and he had three older brothers.

Try this game when your child is two and a half, three and four to see how his ideas change. It's clear that while most three-year-olds can't do it because they think the person they are playing with already knows where the coin is, by the time he is four or so your child will have learnt the truth. And at this moment he will also realize that it is possible to lie.

Abi (aged four and a half) speaks

❝ *My mum read me the story of Little Red Riding Hood. It's kind of exciting and scary 'cause I don't like woods. The trees are all big and it rains and drips go down my neck! Anyway … Little Red Riding Hood – she's called that 'cause she wears a red hood! That's funny! Anyway, Little Red Riding Hood goes to see her granny and the granny isn't in bed it's a BIG BAD WOLF! And it's going to EAT HER UP! YUM YUM. And then Little Red Riding Hood is ate up and she's in the wolf's tummy and a big man with a saw comes in and cuts the wolf up and Little Red Riding Hood and her granny both jump out! But I knew it was a wolf and I think it's stupid 'cause Little Red Riding Hood knew it was a wolf … because it was.* ❞

Once your child understands that other people have different ideas to his, he can start not only to lie, but to develop conscious (and clever) strategies to get what he wants. One strategic young child I know asked very kindly whether he could carry his mother's shopping. The bag wasn't heavy so his mother said 'yes', little knowing what her clever son had in store. He then put the bag very gently in the buggy, beside his sleeping brother. Then with a triumphant smile he held up his arms, pointing out with faultless logic that now his mother didn't have the bag, she could carry him!

But there is more to thinking than logic and strategy. Looking after the body is also important. A thousand years ago the Romans

needed plenty of quick-thinking men and women to run their empire and fight their wars, and had a saying: *mens sana in corpore sano,* a healthy mind in a healthy body. A thousand years later, research shows how right they were. If your child is well exercised, eats plenty of healthy food and gets a good night's sleep, he will work better and feel better. Only with plenty of sleep and good food will your child soar, and exercise releases endorphins – natural opiates which increase happiness and confidence, improving not only the mood but also upgrading the mind.

A DAY IN THE LAB

Psychologists have tested the theory that exercise makes us think better and found it to be true. They took a number of people of all ages and asked them to do nothing physical for a day and then come into the gym for a test. First they were asked to write down as many nouns as possible beginning with C, F and L. One minute was allowed for each letter. The letters are of high, medium and lower frequency, with the last letter the most difficult. Then the volunteers did twenty-five minutes of energetic exercise, either on the cycling, running or rowing machines, and, after cooling down for fifteen minutes, they were tested again, this time with a minute for each of the letters P, R and W – again letters of high, medium and lower frequency.

The result was amazing. After exercise the scores went up, and the tricky third letter was up the most. That's because exercise makes the blood race, brain chemicals are released and the brain cells fire up, making you more alert. Some people believe that the effect is cumulative; the more exercise you do, the better your mind works!

Thinking can be superficial, profound, fast or slow, but above all it is intensely personal; though we all have the same tools, each of us uses them differently. Society may prize quick thinking and rapid decision-taking, but not everyone conforms.

AL'S STORY

There is an elephant trap waiting for the over-zealous parent, as my old friend Margo discovered. Al was a placid three-year-old boy, with a round face and a big smile – what could be nicer? But Margo felt that her delightful son was not very clever; he seemed dazed by the world and didn't seem to 'get it' as fast as other kids, so she decided to get him up to speed. But Al was not constitutionally a speedy boy and he quickly got angry with his mother because of all the activities she wanted him to do, and communicated his disdain in a simple but effective way. Every time she tried to persuade him to do an activity, he turned away. If she insisted, he moved away, and if she really insisted he stood stock still and cried. Margo was a loving mother and she got the message. Al didn't want to move fast, he wanted to go at his own pace. History proved that Al had got it right, as our insightful children often do. Al wasn't lacking in motivation or brains, he was simply a thoughtful boy whose brain worked exceedingly methodically and was easily over-stimulated. Much to his and Margo's pleasure – and, I hate to say it, surprise – he became a talented musician and is now aiming for a first-class maths degree. And Margo learnt an important and long-lasting lesson – never underestimate your child's character or his need to think at his own speed.

WHAT YOU CAN DO ... for all children

- Your child is very logical, so if you pay attention to the mistakes he makes you will find that there is always an interesting reason behind them. A kid who is encouraged to think will go on getting cleverer. (See p.68 for scaffolding techniques.)

- Your child loves to think, and as he discovers the laws of the universe he will not just accept the rules, he'll want to know why. Thinking about cause and effect is good, and the world – with you ready to interpret – is a great teacher. Watch what happens, for instance, when he is exposed to the consequences of his practical actions. Whether good (he gets something he wants) or bad (he doesn't!), he shoulders the responsibility and his learning is never forgotten. And he's not the only one who can ask 'Why?'! You'll find that asking 'Why?' and 'How?' back will deliver an exciting glimpse into his inner world.

- For many children, creativity is the better half of thinking. Children are naturally experimental and can be wild in their imagination. Creativity provides freedom to think the impossible and to imagine different worlds. Young children can be very rule-bound, so help them jump out of their certainties and be enthusiastically wrong!

- It takes a while to learn how to sustain conversation, and your child can get so embroiled in what he is doing he won't want to be interrupted, especially since he may not be able to pause in an activity, deal with a disturbance and go back seamlessly to what he was doing. So be patient and respect his thinking time.
- Choose or invent games that involve all sorts of thinking, using stories, toys and activities.
- Encourage all children to look after themselves, and get plenty of exercise, sleep, good food and time to think.

Thinking is about deduction and guesswork, refining and flexing ideas, adjusting and adapting rules to fit the facts, growing intelligence and building knowledge. Next I will show you how all these work in practice, examining number power, the creativity intrinsic to art and music, and, first and foremost, the incredible power of words.

Word Power

Your baby starts to learn to speak while still in the womb and arrives in the world miraculously primed to turn sounds and feelings into words. Why? Because communication is fundamental and the power of words will fashion your child's life like nothing else.

Most of us think we communicate rather well, but do we? Communication is one of the most difficult skills we learn. In a typical day, most people take part in conversations where there are misunderstandings, hustling and interruption, slights given and offence taken. In Britain alone, many millions of pounds are spent every year on training managers to communicate effectively with their employees. Unsurprisingly, simple words like 'thank you' can be unexpectedly potent!

DO IT YOURSELF

We did an experiment in a crowded London shop to test the potency of one of our most common words, the power word 'because'.

We sent an actor called James into a busy grocery store and asked him to jump the queue using different techniques to persuade people to let him go in front of them. First he tried to push in without giving a reason:

James:	Can I jump the queue?
Man:	No!
James	*(to another customer):*
	Excuse me, can I jump ahead of you?
Man:	Do what? No, I'm being served!
	Next James invented a plausible reason:
James:	Can I jump in? – it's because I'm in a rush.
Man:	Yes, OK.
James:	Excuse me, could you let me in?
	'Cause I'm in a rush.
Woman:	All right, if you're quick.

*Then James decided to try some silly
explanations:*

James: Excuse me, can I jump ahead? Because I hate queues.
Woman: Erm … OK.
James: Please can I jump the queue? It's because it's my
           birthday next week.
Man: Yes, I suppose that's all right.
           *It turns out that giving a reason, any reason, is
           surprisingly persuasive. Try it yourself!*

No other means of communication is as versatile and precise as language, but although your newborn baby has a long way to go, she doesn't start from scratch.

Fascinating facts about language and newborns

Your newborn baby already knows more than you might think about language.

- She prefers her native language, which she has heard in the womb.
- She can tell the difference between English and Swahili.
- She knows the cadences of her own language.
- She knows how to distinguish each small sound. For instance, she recognizes the difference between 'ba' and 'pa', and 'ke' and 'ge'.
- The noises she makes already contain some elements of speech.
- By the time she is about six weeks old, your baby will be cooing and gurgling and, if you listen hard, you will probably even hear her beginning to experiment with different vowel sounds.

Gesture and, indeed, the simple sign language that some parents teach their very young children can help a child communicate specific needs and reduce frustration. But the guessing game of gesture and surmise is transformed as soon as she can talk, and most children find learning language a blessed relief, after all that mystery and misunderstanding. It is not surprising we want to speed the process up. Fortunately, as children are dead set on learning, most parents do the right thing completely automatically!

A DAY IN THE LAB

Teaching your child to speak what is, after all, a brand-new language isn't difficult because all children want to learn. Mothers and other adults will often talk to their babies in a high-pitched, sing-song voice, which research has shown is very helpful. This is called 'parentese' and is a good way to talk to babies, as the tone and repetition is comforting. In its overemphatic way, parentese teaches the rhythms of conversation, distinguishing words and cadences that signal the end of one message and the beginning of the next. So nonsense like 'Who's my little gorgeous, then? Aren't you just the loveliest thing? You are a lovely little one, aren't you?' does something important. Very soon your baby will have familiarized herself to the rhythms of language and you can graduate to more complex speech.

Different children learn language at different rates, and the timing has not got a lot to do with intelligence or later success. Some children understand a lot but don't talk much, while others learn a word and use it in their next sentence. Just as teenagers mature at anything from twelve to sixteen but all get there in the end, so some babies speak their first words at nine months, and others not until well into their second year, when the floodgates open. There are various reasons for fast progression: some children love language, some parents and siblings talk a lot and some babies mature early. By the same token, there are various reasons for delays: some children mature late, some are not spoken to very much or people speak 'for' them, and some just don't think speaking is necessary if gestures and noises work as well. Twins and triplets often develop their own language and don't learn to speak properly until much later.

The Stages of Language Development

Like the average suit that doesn't fit anyone snugly, the average pace of language development won't accurately reflect that of your child! The different stages are likely, however, to follow each other in this order:

- When she is just a few months old, your child will know all the basic sounds – called phonemes – that make up the language. Ah, ba, cah, etc. – all are recognized.
- First words arrive any time after eight months. The first may be one they have heard a lot, like 'baba' or 'cat', or even several words made into one, like ''ereyouare', but others arrive like a bolt from the blue. I know one child whose first word was, very distinctly, 'crow'! No one knew why she chose to start with that!
- By the time your baby is eleven months old, she is likely to understand 'Mummy', 'Daddy' and about seventy other words,

and twelve phrases like 'Stop it' or 'Give me a hug,' and she will be learning an extraordinary ten new words a day, many of them nouns. Small children hunt for nouns because they contain the secret of the subject.

- By fifteen months your child may only need to hear a word once before she uses it. She knows the difference between 'the car' and 'a car', and appreciates the importance of word order – vital, of course, if she is to understand that there is a difference between 'You eat chicken' and 'Chickens eat you'!

A fascinating fact about accent

Your baby is born with the ability to detect the hundred and fifty different sounds from 'ng' to 'sh' that language is made up of, and can even hear the subtle differences between Chinese accents. But just six months later she jettisons the sounds she doesn't need and after that she can't hear all the subtle nuances of pronunciation worldwide. It is at this stage that her easy capacity to absorb any accent in any language has disappeared. It is said that perfect pronunciation needs to be learnt at your mother's knee, syntax and grammar can wait seven years, but vocabulary can be learnt for ever!

- At one and a half your child may be able to understand complex commands, although she can not yet give them as the part of the brain that deals with speech is still growing fast. And if she doesn't have the right word, she'll invent a new one. 'Tracoter' was one coined by my son for tractor and came into general use in our family.
- By twenty-two months your child will be combining ideas in speech – 'Look cat!' – sometimes in bizarre and comical combinations, and she will be learning fifteen new words every day.
- Almost all two-year-olds understand almost everything you say, but even when they don't, they rote learn, sometimes singing TV jingles without understanding a single word!

- By two your child will also talk a lot more, with a vocabulary ranging from fifty to two hundred words. In fact, the most linguistically inclined may have five hundred words in her lexicon! This is the year when the gap between fast and slow learners begins to close. It is also the year when girls start to – slightly – out-perform boys.
- And two-year-olds still make lots of mistakes. See if your child over-extends words, using, for instance, 'doll' for all soft toys or 'dad' for all men. And see if she under-extends, using the word 'mug' to mean 'my favourite mug'. I have found that the latter is harder to spot!
- Two-year-olds' sentences grow with them. At the beginning of the year they may contain only two words; by the end they will be handling long sentences with clauses.
- Your two-year-old will also be absorbing thousands of double meanings – there, their, they're, hair, hare, the list is endless but won't faze your child for long.

A fascinating fact about gestures

Young children use gestures naturally; they wave, smile, wriggle with delight, hide their head when scared, reach out for what they want and turn towards you as a question, asking 'Is this safe?', helping themselves out when they don't have the words. By the time she is one, you'll be able to direct your child's gaze just by looking at something yourself. Some children are so good at making gestures they lose the will to learn language! As we get older we tend to restrict gesticulation, especially in northern countries, coming to rely heavily on words alone. But gesture is still important, and adults who use their hands as well as their voices are heard more easily and listened to more respectfully.

- By the time she is nearly three, your child will start to search for different words to convey a message if you don't understand her the first time, instead of loudly repeating something you don't understand and never will!
- Three-year-olds will incorporate suffixes like '-ing' and get past and future tenses right.
- At three, your child will also begin to negotiate the minefield of complex language conventions. For instance, if she says 'Look at that lady!' you will think at the very least that the lady must be doing something odd. But if she is, in fact, referring to your well-

loved sister, you'll be surprised at her being called 'that lady', even though your child is linguistically correct.

- By the time she is four, your child will be borrowing phrases and whole sentences from her teachers, parents, siblings, friends, the movies and TV, and possibly doing bad American accents to comic effect!
- Four-year-olds are also at the peak of 'fast mapping', learning new words with a rapidity that may bring their vocabulary up to several thousand words – and their grammar is almost always correct.
- Four-year-olds may also be starting to read. The first job is to let them understand that the strange squiggles on paper have meaning and can be deciphered. Then, learning by association, they can put word and letter shapes together. A four-year-old also has sufficient fine motor skills to draw the letters of her name, albeit shakily!

Child of Our Time children speak

The *Child of Our Time* children were four and a half when we found out which letters they knew.

Megan:	I know that's M because that's in my name. My mum has two 'Ms in her name. But I don't know the other letters. Except P and K – and M.
William:	A, B, C, Dippy Duck, Eddy Elephant, Fireman Fred, Golden Girl, Hairy Hat Man, Jumping Jim, Lucy Lamplady, M for Naughty Nick, P, W, T, O, V for violets, W for William, and then – don't know.
Taliesen:	That's 4 *[in fact it's an A]* and that's 3, isn't it? *[in fact it's a P]*.

As you can see, four-year-old children vary enormously in their knowledge of letters, it all depends how much they've been taught and how interested they are – but not how intelligent they are!

- Five-year-olds will be reading simple books and writing, though rarely with accurate spelling. They will also be talking more gracefully and using adjectives and adverbs more fluently. Much of this will be automatic, and your child will have a staggering three to five thousand words at her disposal!

- Six-year-olds will read more skilfully and grammatically and spell many words correctly. They will also start the more abstract task of thinking consciously about which words would better explain their thoughts.
- By the time your child is seven, she will be reading and writing more fluently and will have enough knowledge of the difference between spoken and written styles to be able to face her first exams with a degree of confidence – I hope!

A fascinating fact about BIG words

Big, unusual words are harder to remember than short ones, even for adults; too many of them will gridlock short-term memory. If you use easy words for difficult ideas and keep long words for easy ideas, your mind will work better! Knowing how a word is made up helps – seeing the meaning of prefixes and suffixes like -ist, -ion, and un- will help make the word feel smaller. Gaining a big vocabulary and using it until it is automatic makes for better thinking, so the best thing to do is use your long words often, until they seem smaller.

DO IT YOURSELF: Language checklist for your two-year-old child

This questionnaire uses a selection of words of varying difficulty. It is not designed to test every word your child might know. Some of the words are difficult so try testing him again in a few months time to see if his vocabulary has grown.

Which, if any, words in the list can your child say? Tick a word he knows even if he says it differently, like tirsty instead of thirsty.

Can he join two or more words together to make a little sentence?

Does he generally understand the names of everyday objects?

Can the family understand what he says?

Most children of two know a lot of the first words, but the other words are more unusual and if he knows a third of those he is doing very well. If he scores lower it may be that he is more interested in doing other things rather than attending to language so try to teach him some more words, concentrating on things he is focused on at the time. But if you are concerned about his language, and if the answer to some of the above questions is 'no' then talk to your health visitor or doctor. It is possible, for instance, that he has hearing problems.

First Words:

Bye/Bye-bye	No	Mummy/Mum	Hot	Shoe
Dog/Doggie	Juice	Up/Carry	Please	Ouch/Ow

Other Words:

Tractor	Car	Book	Milk	Coat
Thank-you	Nose	Cloud	Rubbish	Plate
Towel	Bed	Settee/Sofa	School	Friend
Man	Shop	Hello/Hi	Draw	Sad
Fit	Find	Rip/Tear	Write	Watch
Gentle	Fast	Thirsty	Last	High
Dry	After	This	Day	Yours
Where	All	Some	Need	If

Some children have a wonderfully rich vocabulary. This doesn't happen by accident. Chatty parents, who enjoy long conversations with their children where new words are offered and learnt, will tend to produce children whose language snowballs. Rhianna's mother does just that.

Tanya and Rhianna speak

Tanya is the mother of three-year-old Rhianna, who is playing with her dolls.

> **Rhianna:** He's a very, very strong man is Ken. He can lift you up, right up, mummy doll, he can lift her as high as he can.
>
> **Tanya:** It's a verbal stream constantly, where she's informing you what's going on, and asking questions. It's non-stop.
>
> **Rhianna:** Look! She can even fly with him.
>
> **Tanya:** I run off at the mouth too – I talk a lot and explain a lot.
>
> **Rhianna:** Ken, you must go in now. It's time for you to get into the car and race away!

Some lucky children learn two – or even more – languages from birth, and as long as they hear either one or the other and don't muddle them up, they benefit from this. The language areas of their brain become richer in connections between nerve cells, and each language offers different ways of thinking with which to appreciate the world.

Vijay speaks

Het lives in an Indian community in north-west London with her grandparents and parents, mum Tejal and dad Vijay, who says:

> **❝** Gujarati is our main language with our relatives at home, but Het will definitely be bilingual by the time she is at school. It is an asset to speak two languages, it means you learn the difference between peoples and understand the qualities of their life. And if you speak their language people will appreciate it and will help you. I think it can make you a more powerful person in the world. **❞**

But sometimes learning to talk can happen frighteningly slowly, and then your child will need some special help.

JACKIE'S STORY

Jackie is one of a number of parents I have met whose child just didn't seem to want to talk. Her son Saul was three but had the language skills of someone much younger and Jackie was worried he might be deaf. A test, however, didn't show any problem there and Jackie was at her wits' end. So what could be the matter? First I talked with Jackie to find out what went on at home. It transpired that Jackie had her own business which she managed in between looking after Saul and his elder brother Aaron. With no childcare, time was short and she tended to talk to the children while doing household chores with the TV on in the background. But she also wanted her children to do well so most of her talking took the form of teaching. Saul's older brother usually answered the questions, so Saul, who wasn't as able, just switched off.

Something had to be done, so, based on research, I suggested a four-point plan. She should set aside at least half an hour every day for quiet play with Saul; he was to choose the activity. She should stop firing questions at him and start describing appreciatively what he was doing, being especially aware of where he was looking. She was to use plenty of words he didn't know but whose meaning was obvious in context and, finally, she was to sit at his level and encourage eye contact so he could do some lip reading if he needed to

– we all understand better if we can see the person who's talking.

Initially Jackie was rather scared of this plan, and it's not surprising. She rarely spent any relaxed time with the children and the pressures of her business made her feel desperate to get up and *do* something. But she stuck with it and the results quickly changed her attitude. Within just a few weeks Saul's interest in language had grown and after a couple of months his language had improved, and, better still, he was engaging enthusiastically in conversation. And he had, at last, learnt to listen for the sounds he wanted to hear, his mum's loving words.

Big changes in language happen at around five years old. The accumulation of life experience, practice with verbal negotiation and looking at books precipitates a dramatic development – learning to read. Reading will take your child into a new world, where fantasies are played out, ideas tested and vicarious experience gained. Reading also triggers the understanding of shades of meaning, because the words are spelt out in many different contexts, generating an implicit understanding of their precise meaning, so the word 'kind' is grouped with others like 'generosity', 'empathy' and 'sympathy' without carrying exactly the same meaning.

Reading and Writing

In my school, teaching reading relied predominantly on learning how to recognize the alphabet and learning the shape of whole words, using helpful first letters plus the context. This was combined with a decision to eschew reading schemes and instead use funny, well-illustrated 'real' books that could be read and enjoyed with adults.

Now there is a greater emphasis on phonics (see below), but children still need to pick up clues from pictures, grammatical rules from speech, known letters and, often, previous knowledge of the book. This is particularly important for English learners because the language is highly irregular so a logical approach to deciphering words can lead nowhere. This is unfortunately true of more than half the one hundred most common English words.

The first words your child learns to read may not be any of the hundred most common, because, just like in speech, she will initially hunt for the nouns, starting with her own name and those of family members. Nouns are easier because they give immediate insight into what the word means, and the shape of a word, associated with an image of the object, makes it easier to recall than more abstract words like 'their'. Words like 'crocodile' crop up in children's picture books far more often than they ever do in adult books, but children love it because it's a nice-looking word linked to a stunning picture!

A fascinating fact about the English language

A friend of mine, the educational psychologist Jonathan Solity, told me about a huge database of 850,000 words that was used to find the most commonly used words in English writing. The average adult knows about twenty thousand words, but just one hundred words form a staggering 53 per cent of our written language.

The crucial 100 words

a, about, after, all, am, an, and, are, as, at, away
back, be, because, big, but, by
call, came, can, come, could
did, do, down
for, from
get, go, got
had, has, have, he, her, here, him, his
I, in, into, is, it
last, like, little, live, look
made, make, me, my
new, next, not, now
of, off, old, on, once, one, other, our, out, over
put
saw, said, see, she, so, some
take, that, the, their, them, then, there, they, this, three, time, to, today, too, two
up, us
very
was, we, were, went, what, when, will, with
you

Over half the words your child needs to know to read any adult book are in this list! All of them are vital for understanding, but less than half obey simple rules of spelling. The rest may need to be learnt by rote and repetition.

Many children have a gift for accepting irregular spellings in language and there are plenty of them to practise on: words like knife, chair, thought, cupboard and bicycle which don't 'sound out' easily. Many children learn to read and write using the alphabet, whole words and common sense without ever having to learn all the basic sounds. But for others, absorbing large numbers of words whole can be too big a mouthful. They need more than the alphabet and native wit; they need a system called phonics, where children are taught to read phonemes.

A fascinating fact about phonemes

Learning phonemes is one good way to help your child learn to read, because most children have an intuitive understanding of the sounds that make up their language, which can be accessed when they are taught letter sounds.

- A phoneme is a single distinct sound, one of forty-two that make up the English language.
- At just one year, your baby can recognize all the phonemes and can even distinguish more subtle differences between sounds – for instance, between the 'l' in leap and the 'l' in deal.
- The task of putting phonemes together to make words is assisted enormously by this early and intuitive knowledge of sounds.
- The difficulty comes with reading and writing, because our twenty-six letters do not match the forty-two phonemes.
- But children are good at guessing and can accept that one phoneme can be represented by more than one letter. For in stance, the phoneme 'k' can be written as 'k', 'c' and 'ck'.
- And children can accept that one letter can indicate several phonemes. For instance, the letter 'A' can represent two phonemes: the 'a' sound in 'cat' and the 'A' sound in 'cake'.
- The small differences in one phoneme, like the 'th' in 'this' and 'th' in 'three', don't fox them for long.

If a child is going to learn to read using phonics it is helpful for her to know that the task isn't simple and that many letters have more than one sound. Knowing this, your child can, and probably will, learn the most common sound of the letter first, but at least she won't be fazed when the rules are broken.

Learning to recognize phonemes linked to a letter or sound and then to blend them together – like cuh-ah-t = cat – can take slow learners some time, but it is a useful skill to have, particularly when you meet a new word, though even then, mistakes can be made. As adults know, they can happen to anyone at any time. At the age of thirty-five a friend of mine was still pronouncing 'plagiarism' phonetically. She only stopped because someone laughed at her!

In a perfect world each sound would be represented by a single letter. But though this is largely true in Italian and Spanish, it is most definitely not the case in English, as the list below demonstrates.

DO IT YOURSELF

Here's a list of the forty-two commonly used phonemes. Have fun thinking up noises that will stick the phoneme sound in your child's head for ever, starting with the simple ones like 'p', 's', 'd', 't', 'i', 'a' and 'n'.

Sound	Spellings	Sound	Spellings
A	table (a), bake (a ... e), train (ai), say (ay)	t	teddy (t)
		U	future (u), use (u ... e), few (ew)
a	bat (a)		
b	bend (b)	u	drum (u), about (a), wagon (u)
k	catch (c), key (k), rack (ck)		
d	door (d)	v	voice (v)
E	me (e), keep (ee), leap (ea), baby (y)	w	wash (w)
		ks/gs	box (x), exam (x)
e	led (e), head (ea)	y	yes (y)
f	film (f), photo (ph)	z	zoo (z), nose (s)
g	golf (g)	OO	soon (oo), truth (u), rude (u ... e), flew (ew)
h	hot (h)		
I	ice (i), kite (i ... e), night (igh), sky (y)		
		oo	book (oo), put (u)
i	sit (i)	oi	foil (oi), toy (oy)
j	joke (j), ledge (dg), gym (g)	ou	out (ou), cow (ow)
l	leg (l)	aw	flaw (aw), caught (au), tall (a)
m	me (m)		
n	no (n), knife (kn)	ar	car (ar)
O	OK (o), joke (o ... e), soap (oa), grow (ow)	sh	show (sh), nation (ti), special (ci)
o	dog (o)	ch	chin (ch), catch (tch)
p	pat (p)	TH	then (th)
kw	quiet (qu)	th	thin (th)
r	road (r), wrong (wr), her (er), stir (ir), blur (ur)	ng	sing (ng), think (n)
		zh	pleasure
s	snake (s), centre (c)		

In the current enthusiasm for phonemes, many of us neglect the next important building block of fluent reading, the morpheme. Morphemes are bits of words that have their own meaning. For instance the prefix 'pre-' means 'before' and is used in words like premature, pre-school and preview. 'Un-' means 'not' in words like unusual, uninteresting and uninviting. There are also suffixes like '-ology', which means 'study of' in words such as geology, psychology and biology, and suffixes that tell us what someone does, such as '-ist' and '-er' (scientist, manicurist, hairdresser and robber). The beauty of morphemes is that they increase vocabulary, because your child need only learn the pieces to be able to deduce the meaning.

Writing is the final stage in learning word power, and begins to come into its own when your child is seven. By then her hand-eye coordination will be well on the way to adult dexterity, but her spelling may seem atrocious! Somehow the spelling she knows from reading doesn't show itself in writing, leading to lots of perfectly logical mistakes.

KATY'S STORY

Katy gave me a piece of paper a few days ago, which came with a lovely anecdote. The paper contained a short story written some months earlier, when Katy was just seven. She loved writing and had dedicated time and energy to this story, which was for her mother. The story was about love.

But when Katy's mother, Liz, received it, she was feeling irritable and, though secretly proud, felt her daughter should learn to spell, so asked her to write it out properly. Instead Katy had a fine old tantrum and was sent to bed.

A few hours later Liz read it again and, in spite of the crazy spelling, recognized that the story was easy to read because Katy was following the rules as best she could and being very logical. In fact, in a more sensible world, Katy's spellings might be absolutely correct. Here it is ...

Love is the best thing in paradise. Ofcourse, the peple that no us love us and we do to. So you see that love is Vere Iipotant. Just the Same as I love my Ante. But were not going to do that sort of love. Were going to do True Love. you see True Love is When Some one See they fole in love Strat Away. Some one and there haart gos ping. and

That night something magical was in the air because when Liz showed the story to her husband Toby they suddenly hugged each other and laughed.

Most children learn to spell using a mix of rote learning, 'sounding out' and visual memory. Fortunately, there are some rules to learn. The three most useful are the magic 'e' that turns a vowel from soft to hard – ah to A as in 'fat' to 'fate', for instance – the fact that 'c' is usually soft when followed by an I, as in 'circus' and 'citizen', and the rhyme 'i before e, except after c', which I still use when in doubt.

WHAT YOU CAN DO ... for all children

- All children are born to talk and those lucky enough to grow up in a talkative household will have heard fifty million words by the time they are three and will have learnt lots of them. The amount of rich conversation babies have with siblings and carers is not related to class or wealth, but rather to the chattiness and child-centredness of the household. Anyone can give their child a love of language if they just take the time to talk, especially if you make use of your child's emerging sense of humour.

- Word power is gained quickly by nine out often of our children, but some find it harder to remember words, formulate sentences or speak without lisping or stammering. What you do can help enormously however old or young your child is, so take time to talk with her one-to-one in a quiet place where you both can relax.

The way you talk to your child can change her understanding. Here are five tips on talking:

1 Look at what your child looks at, get to her level and say what is actually happening and she will learn quickly. Children love to communicate when they are certain you are talking to them and are told about things they can see, hear or feel.

2 'Scaffold' communication (see p.68) by acknowledging your child's contribution and then offering her exciting new words and ideas.

3 Speak clearly, use gestures and let your child see you – lip reading is part of learning to talk. Keep sentences short, using vocabulary your child will understand.

4 Sing or recite rhymes and songs, repeating words and sounds together, look at books and pictures together and encourage her to have a go, without worrying to much about accuracy.

5 Remember, she learns from you! Silence breeds silence, chattiness breeds talk and affection breeds communication.

The way you listen to your child can also change her world. Here are five tips on listening:

1 Consider your child's ideas with respect.

2 Be patient, she may need to do some thinking before she puts her ideas into words.

3 Use reflective listening, repeating back what she has said in your own words, correcting inaccuracies casually; that way you'll encourage further explanation and find out if you really understand her.

4 If she asks a question, check out whether she has her own answer before you give yours. It may open a little window into her world.

5 Remember how special she is! And if she knows you are listening with all your attention, she will tell you her secrets.

WHAT YOU CAN DO ... for your baby

- Talk! Talk! Talk! The more words your baby hears, the better. Action games like 'Round and round the garden', 'This little piggie' and nursery rhymes, lullabies with repetitive language, made-up chants like 'Bit bat bot, pit pat pot' – they are all great, helping children to learn words, distinguish sounds, enjoy rhythm. Reading picture books with your child at nine months will help her do better at school at seven – and all of these lovely games pay dividends for ever.

WHAT YOU CAN DO ... for toddlers

- Listen and talk! Extend her, give her lovely new words to play with, let her enjoy names, and set up a regular book-time. Pop-up, waterproof, board, audio, smelly or just the regular words and pictures – any book will do.
- Communicate. Use pointing, eye contact, listening, smiles, gestures and hugs. If you're responsive she'll grow in communication confidence.
- Tell stories. Encourage her to tell stories too, be they true or false, funny, pointless, or crazy stories that make everyone laugh.

WHAT YOU CAN DO ... for older children

- Play games. Fantasy play encourages experiments with speech; the Instruction game with cards – saying 'jump', 'sing', 'groan', 'shout' – teaches expressiveness; word-order games, where sentences are re-ordered, can be hilarious; spelling Snap is good for seven-year-olds and old favourites like 'I-Spy' work wonders on car journeys.
- Learn sounds. Start with the regular ones – t, s, p, a, n, i – using three-letter words like 'it', 'tip', 'tin', 'pin', 'sip', and 'at', 'sat', 'pat', 'pan', 'tan'. Play with rhymes and rhythms.
- Read. Children love books with a good story, great pictures and familiar, spoken English, and they love to be stretched, so keep your child at the tipping point where she knows some of the words and gets to learn new ones.
- Write. Rules help, so do visualizing and sounding words. Remind your child of the magic 'e', the 'i' before 'e' except after 'c' rule, the soft 'c' that prefaces 'i' (and tell her that they occasionally don't work so she isn't surprised at irregularities). And praise her when she's a good guesser.
- Love words! Get your child to read road signs for safety, books for fun and packets for information; stick words on objects to help with spelling, copy shopping lists to help with writing and send letters and birthday cards to friends and family.

Number Power

There is so much written about language learning and so little about logic and maths that it is hard to escape the thought that people are frightened of numbers! But logic and maths are a crucial part of our life and it is important to be able to manipulate them well.

There is an extraordinary fissure between learning maths at school, which all too often leaves children and adults with the sense that they don't quite understand it, and the complex mathematical ideas that we use every day quite automatically. In a recent poll nearly 80 per cent of people confessed to being a maths dunce, but almost everyone knows about money, and can work out how much they have to pay. Maths doesn't have to be difficult. It relies fundamentally on simple concepts and obvious logic, and if your child is confident about numbers he is en route to becoming a mathematical whiz!

SHINICHI SUZUKI'S STORY

The famous violin teacher Shinichi Suzuki was concerned with all sorts of learning, and one day he saw his young nephew being punished for forgetting how to count to ten and decided to teach numbers to this six-year-old learning-disabled boy so they could never be forgotten.

First, Suzuki watched as the boy tried to count and quickly noticed that four and seven were particular stumbling blocks, and he saw that each time they came up his mother scolded.

Suzuki took a piece of cardboard and quietly made a dice, writing only fours and sevens on the faces. Then he invited the boy to join him. They rolled the dice, Suzuki called out the numbers and laughed and said he had won. Suzuki's enthusiasm was infectious and after a few minutes the boy shouted 'four' and 'seven' too. This time they both won! They continued to play and sometimes Suzuki shouted the wrong number so the boy could correct him. Ten entertaining minutes past and during that time sevens and fours became, as Suzuki says, the boy's favourite numbers – and when later tested by his mother the boy shouted loudest and longest when he reached four and seven.

Suzuki tells us that even if a parent is overflowing with love but uses angry and impatient methods, their child will not develop a skill.

Some of us are so de-skilled as children we have problems with maths for the whole of our lives. So how can we help our children?

The Stages of Number Development

- All children have an innate understanding of numbers that starts in the womb when they hear the rhythm of their mother's heart, and have the ability to recognize groups of one and two, probably three and possibly even more.

A DAY IN THE LAB

In the year 2000 some of the *Child of Our Time* parents played groups of 'beeps' to their children in the womb in order to familiarize the unborn child with the sequence one beep, two beeps and three beeps. The babies remembered that sequence, just as they remembered the music they had heard in the womb. But I wondered if they could abstract the numbers and recognize them in pictorial form, as one, two or three objects. Professor Annette Karmiloff-Smith helped me find out by sitting the newborn babies in front of the number pictures and recording what they gazed at. It was fascinating to be there, especially when Annette told us that our babies looked very intently when the numbers of objects grew in their appointed order, which suggested thay they really did recognize the sequence. It was exciting to think that this was their first mathematical experience and we all hoped it presaged well for the future!

- Very young children have a sense of number. By four months babies stare in surprise if they watch two things go behind a screen and find that only one – or three – are there when the screen is moved.
- At one year old, with his sense of number growing, your child will spot the gaps if you move something away and notice when you add something. This is the starting point for subtraction and addition.
- At two years old children can usually count to three and your child will be inordinately proud of his age! He'll recognize

geometric shapes like triangles and circles and will even begin to think about sharing things out fairly between people or dolls.

- Three-year-olds can share things out one to one – or, sometimes, two things to one person. Your child will use number language like 'one', 'two', 'three', 'lots', 'more' and 'hundreds' and will ask 'how many?' But he will still be muddled about how to share fairly objects like Lego if there are two bits stuck together.

- Children of four can count to ten and even twenty, and play easy number games. Four-year-olds can also manage quite complex number tasks, distributing single and double Lego bricks fairly between children using one-to-one correspondence.

- Five-year-olds can count to twenty or more, and can often start from any number and count forward or backwards. They can read simple numbers and will be willing to estimate how many bricks go into a tower. A few children of five can even sort 2p and 1p coins so each child receives the same amount of money, but this skill usually emerges at around six. Five-year-olds can also understand a very important fact – that counting leads to a final number, which represents a certain number of objects. This is called the cardinal principle.

- Six-year-old children can count to a hundred and do simple additions in their heads, especially if the sums are illustrated. For instance, a picture of a road with several people placed along it, and the number of metres between them labelled, helps children to understand the sum and add the distances.

- Seven-year-olds can understand fractions if they are given not as abstract concepts but as one-to-one correspondence tasks – for instance, between children and pizzas, so three children and one

pizza means one-third each – though they might need help writing the fraction down. And there is another thing that tends to come automatically to anyone over eleven but can be understood earlier. Take a sum like $9 + 5 - 5 = ?$ Young children do this sequentially, painstakingly adding the second number and then taking away the third. But some seven-year-olds realize that the equation can be solved easily because $+5$ and -5 simply cancel each other out.

- Ultimately your child will be able to manipulate numbers easily, abstracted from any practical task, and once he can do that he will be able to transfer his skills across the widest possible range of problems and come out with marvellous and accurate answers to calculations ranging from the cost of his shopping to the size of the cosmos.

Young children's maths is based on digesting four rules.
- First that numbers have a stable order. When you name animals, 'sheep', 'cow', 'lion' and 'fox' can be in any order, but counting has to start with one and go straight on. One, two, eight, five just won't work!
- The second rule is that a number is not an object or the property of an object like colour or shape; it is the property of a set of things, which can be anything: sweets, dogs or things on the table.
- The third is the cardinal principle, stating that a group of objects can be counted in any order, as long as each object is counted only once. The last number is the number of things in the group.
- And finally there is the one-to-one principle, where there is correspondence both between numbers and objects – with each object linking to a number – and between either side of an equation. Children naturally use the one-to-one principle, for instance when allocating sweets between several people. Sharing fairly lays the basis for multiplication and division.

A DAY IN THE LAB

The educationalist Jonathan Solity has not only worked on language, he has spent years finding out the best way to teach maths to young children. This is what he advises:
- Children can be muddled by terminology, so teachers and parents should stick to using just one term for addition (e.g. 'plus') and subtraction (e.g. 'minus') to avoid confusion. Once the mathematical concepts are well understood you can use a range of words such as 'add' and 'take away'.

- Children learn better if they concentrate on one skill at a time
  – once your child has mastered one he can go on to the next.
- Giving him simple 'mental maths' practice to do in his head can
  help fix ideas. Keep the sessions short and enjoyable. Little and
  often is the key to effective help.
- Give your child one key rule, known as the equity principle
  – that the = sign means that each side of an equation must be
  balanced. As soon as a child understands that, he will be able to
  work out why some answers are right and others wrong. For
  instance, many of Jonathan's five-year-old children could work
  out $1111+111111=10$ 'because we added ten lines'. Once your
  child has this concept firmly in his head he will be able to learn
  to manipulate fractions and multiplications much more easily.

Some children rote-learn rules, and find out what they mean after
they have used them in the abstract. But the majority of children
find the abstract nature of rules off-putting and learn the other way
round, achieving mathematical insights by solving problems.

And just a very few don't even need telling …

Calvin speaks

Calvin is a seven-year-old boy with a good imagination which he
uses to satisfy his many scientific interests, including a remarkable
grasp of maths. His mother, Helen, discussed with Calvin what he
'sees' in his mind when he calculates sums.

Calvin:	I can see everything in a number line; every number from one to a zillion. If it goes further than a hundred then I make the line longer. It's just a black and white line with normal-sized writing on it.
Helen:	So what if you get a sum like fifty-two plus seventeen?
Calvin:	I see it on the line, $52 + 10 + 7$ – it gets to 69.
Helen:	How far can you go?
Calvin:	Well, I can't see it if it's a zillion!! But I think I can get pretty much close up to that.
Helen:	So what about dividing – what's fifteen divided by three?

Calvin	(*immediately*): Five.
Helen:	So how did you know that?
Calvin:	Oh Mu-um. That's just so obvious.

A DAY IN THE LAB: Maths, music and finger fun!

There is a piece of research that suggests that children who have a longer ring finger than index finger may be better with numbers!

The reason seems to be to do with testosterone. Though boys and girls all get some testosterone in the womb, it's usually boys who get the most and they tend to have longer ring fingers and are often better at maths, while girls, who tend to get less testosterone and have longer index fingers, usually have better word power.

But the gender difference is far from a rule. There are lots of girls with longer ring fingers who are also great at maths, whereas the boys with longer index fingers can – and do – become great wordsmiths.

Testosterone and oestrogen levels in the womb, and ring- and index-finger length are also linked with musicianship and sporting prowess; according to research, professional footballers tend to have the longest index fingers of all!

While most children, taught well and allowed to experiment with maths using real problems, will develop their mathematical confidence, there are a few people who are completely unable to get it. They have dyscalculia.

Paul Moorcraft speaks

Paul Moorcraft is a man with a surprising problem. He's a professor of journalism, an author and a war correspondent; he was also an instructor at the UK's most famous military school and worked for the British government's Ministry of Defence. But, although he's one of life's super achievers, there's something he can't do … Paul has dyscalculia, a sort of number blindness.

❝ *If you give me a million pounds I couldn't tell you what my phone number is, or even my Pin number, which makes life rather difficult.*

I can recognize individual numbers, but when they are put together – like a phone number or on a train timetable – I have difficulty in seeing them, I can't copy them or even hear them properly. It affects me every single day. I have to get other people to write down phone numbers for me because 50 per cent of the time I get them wrong. I look at them, then I turn away and I can't remember.

I didn't know when I was a child that I had this condition and I used to wonder, 'What the hell's wrong with me?' Luckily I was very bright and my teachers just thought I was lazy. I've spent hundreds of hours working out how to hide it. After all, you can't say to employers or girl-friends 'I can't count,' they would get rid of you straight away!

Luckily I can do geometry by seeing the shapes, so I just scraped through my O-level maths by a whisker which meant I could ap-ply for university, which was great because I'd thought I'd never have a career. It was especially difficult working at the MoD where my office and the safe had combination locks and you weren't al-lowed to write anything down. But I did, of course, or made up plausible reasons for other people to open the safe. But cov-ering it up obsessed me and eventually it became too difficult. I came out about it a few years ago because it's important other people don't go through the same thing. And I coined a slogan for the dyscalculia campaign: 'Just because I can't count doesn't mean I don't count!'

OK. Now, we're at the bank, and this is my worst nightmare, because I'd rather have my toenails pulled out than try to get money out of the ATM.

Up to one in forty of the population may suffer from dyscalculia to some extent, and scientists have shown that a part of the brain is under-developed in those people. However, it is fatally easy to mix dyscalculia up with the country's pervasive lack of confidence with numbers. People with dyscalculia generally find it very hard to remember numbers. Dyscalculics tend to mix up number orders, sometimes adding extra zeros, and may have great difficulty with everyday activities like dealing with money, reading dice and using Pin numbers. This is very different from those of us who just don't get on with maths.

WHAT YOU CAN DO ... for babies

- Sing counting songs and rhymes like 'One, two, three, four, five, once I caught a fish alive ...' and 'This little piggy went to market ...', and play lost and found games with different numbers of toys so your baby learns to like numbers, becomes familiar with what two, three or more objects look like and begins to see how the picture changes when things are taken away or added.

WHAT YOU CAN DO ... for toddlers

- Your child can get used to the names of small numbers by counting on his fingers to help with laying the table, advising you on how to divide a cake, or creating new shapes out of cardboard. He will be into maths because it's a crucial part of his world.
- Tell stories with numbers and mathematical problems in them. These don't have to be difficult!
- Geometry is likely to be your toddler's forte – building little towers, fitting shapes into their place and working out the properties of balls, pyramids, rectangles, triangles and cubes. Tell him the names of these shapes – he might enjoy knowing them!

Sanjay speaks

Sanjay: I have four dogs. One, Two, Three, Four! That's number four – the old dog. That's number three. And number two has gone out of the room!

Sanjay's mother: So how many dogs are in here now?

Sanjay: One, Three and Four.

Sanjay's mother: Why don't you count them again?

Sanjay *(exasperated)*: One, Three, Four.

WHAT YOU CAN DO ... for older children

- Be enthusiastic about numbers. Have a laugh. Give your child as many grapes as there are days in the week. Ask him to count on his fingers and toes, count out shopping bags, count apples, count the number of steps to get to bed – count anything, in fact. Estimate numbers and quantities – of peas, minutes, ladders, boxes, the universe. Arrange objects (pens and pencils or matches) in rows of fives and tens or threes and twos so he can visualize them.
- Collect a group of things together and get your child to count them; mix them up, take away or add some, ask him to guess how many there are and count again. Use dominoes or play games with dice to help him recognize patterns of individual numbers at a glance. Facility with numbers and good guesswork will come fast and he'll quickly come to love the power of abstraction that numbers give him.
- Use the basis of all maths – one-to-one correspondence, sharing bricks, sweets, books and toys with different people. Your child can help you, putting flowers into different vases, giving each plant a cupful of water, adding a squirt of washing-up liquid into each saucepan. As he gets older, show him different coins and see if he can work out how to give everyone the same value. Even young children can do these sums because they know all about fairness. They can even do fractions if they want everyone to get a fair portion of an orange or a cake!
- Tell stories that involve calculations – stories can work up an emotional force that invites children to think hard. For instance, you could tell a dramatic story where there's only a certain number of bricks to make a castle, or you could find out if a rescue can be effected if the hero runs twenty miles there and back to find the magic potion and his boots will only take him fifty miles – is that enough? And if you run out of your own conundrums there are books to read with your children, and children's TV programmes to watch together.
- Finally, show how you love numbers – millions of miles, infinite numbers of stars, just one of him.

CLIVE

AO

Art and Music

Sound and light explode into our mind the moment we are born. We experience them directly with our senses. Their power is incontestable. No wonder pictures and music are so important to us.

Pictures and music eclipse word power and number power and even the act of thinking. Sound and light are not created by humans but by nature. They set off memory, they fill our emotions and they are immediately accessible.

A fascinating fact about the power of pictures

The question is – what is a box?

You will know all about this box – its shape, its function, its identity – by looking at it for a tiny fraction of a second. So how long does it take to get a sense of it through language?

A box has four sides made up of four rectangles or squares. Each of the opposing sides must be the same size and shape, though the relation between the height, width and depth can vary. This box is silver coloured and is probably about 15 cm by 10 cm by 4 cm. It is decorated with blue butterflies, and has a lid … Well you can see how easy it is to see a box and how hard to describe it in all its detail!

All concrete objects are easier to see than to describe, and children even understand more abstract things, like emotions, if there is a picture to give them shape and form.

This is why children need picture books. Imagine what a mess you would make trying to describe a crocodile! But once we have a picture of something in our mind we can conjure it up at a moment's notice.

DO IT YOURSELF

Take a piece of paper and a pen. Shut your eyes tightly and draw an elephant.

My friends of all ages drew elephants – and here they are.

Aren't they wonderful? And perfectly recognizable as elephants. They even have character. You have almost certainly learnt what an elephant is like from pictures, only later seeing the real thing, but to re-create it without being able to see what you are doing is testimony to the accuracy of your inner eye. Imagine what you would expect an elephant to be like had you only heard about it. Surely it would never have been so real, so textured.

Like pictures, music has an immediacy that makes us able to remember many tunes without effort and re-create them from memory without thinking. The growth of artistic and musical ability starts very early and the developmental shifts in both are uncannily similar.

The Newborn

- Your child hears her first noises in the womb. By the time she is born she will know her mother's voice and be lulled to sleep by the steady beat of her mother's heart. It becomes her theme tune, a steady, soothing backdrop to her daily life. She also sees her first shadowy images in the womb – a fact any pregnant mother can establish by shining a strong light on her belly – if your baby's awake, she wriggles!
- As soon as she is born, your child opens her eyes to see and hear. She will give equal importance to everything around her, be it a slight noise in the distance or the gentle movement of a shadow across a wall. Amazingly she is even better at spotting small differences in bits of music than her parents.

A DAY IN THE LAB

As you have already heard, children learn music so easily they can even do it in the womb!

We tested some newborn babies and discovered that they had learnt the theme tunes of the TV soaps their mothers watched while pregnant. This test has also been done on a grand scale and all the babies tested remembered the tune well after they were born, responding more positively to jingles they had heard in the womb than to other music. More women of childbearing age watch TV soaps than any other section of the population, and I have calculated from audience statistics that 50 per cent of all newborn babies are likely to know at least one of the top three theme tunes by heart! Advertising seems to work from a very early age.

The One-Year-Old

- One-year-olds start to sing tuneless melodies and hit things to make rhythmic noises, and as soon as they can hold a pen they scribble. These first attempts are less about art and more about making a mark on the world, and once your child realizes she can use drawing materials, nothing will stop her. But first, she has to develop some fine motor skills, and this takes time.

A fascinating fact about loud music

We entered the musical arena again when we tested the *Child of Our Time* children's musical preferences when they were just a year old. We found that the majority of our boys went for loud rock, while most of the girls preferred softer music. The reason for this is probably that baby girls tend to have more acute senses, and can perceive quieter sounds, subtler scents and a softer touch than boys.

The Two-Year-Old

- The scribbles of two-year-olds aren't much clearer than those of
  one-year-olds, but now they start to be named, most likely as a
  result of parents and siblings asking what it is! As a result your
  child will realize she is expected to be drawing something real,
  and that she has to build her technical skills.
- By the time she is two, your child is likely to have heard well
  over a thousand hours of music and shows how much she enjoys
  it by moving. In fact, two-year-olds usually dance to music more
  than three-year-olds.

The Three-Year-Old

- Drawing has become purposeful! Your child will try to make
  circles and may put patterns inside the circles and then tell you
  all about them. Gradually her drawings will become more human,
  faces with hair sticking out and oval heads. She may even
  start drawing people with arms coming out of their heads.
  Some people think children do this because they look at themselves – hold your arms right out and you'll see what I mean!
- Given space, your child will enjoy messing about making
  different noises. At the same time she's hearing even more
  music. Some three-year-olds spend most of their days with background music and even the least music-oriented families often
  have the radio on for several hours a day.

A fascinating fact about perfect pitch

Your baby is almost certainly born with perfect pitch. Pitch can be an important dimension if you are to speak a musical language such as Chinese, but English is not very tuneful and in the world of the developing brain where 'use it or lose it' is law, perfect pitch is usually discarded during the first few years of life. But maybe, if you play your child nursery songs and other musical pieces as often as you talk to her, she just might keep her perfect pitch for ever.

- And now your child can start to attempt more purposeful music, banging a tambourine rhythmically or tapping single notes on the piano. But, however well three-year-olds can learn to play, singing in tune is another matter. Young children tend to blur techniques for talking with those for singing and the result – cacophony!

The Four-Year-Old

- What happens if you ask your child to draw a cup, turned so that the handle is invisible? She will almost certainly still draw the handle. That's because she is drawing what she knows is true, rather than simply what she can see. By the same token, she may still find it hard to draw something from someone else's point of view, because she still thinks that other people see what she sees.
- Her musical ability is growing and she may get a passion for certain CDs. My four-year-old god-daughter played *My Fair Lady* non-stop for months, driving her mother mad. At the same time, her vocal chords developed and she began to sing in tune, so maybe it served a useful purpose. At this age your child will enjoy musical instruments – they will be used especially often if you play with them too.

The Five-Year-Old

- At last, drawing things are intellectually realistic is possible, though your child is still in thrall of what she knows rather than what she sees. At six, my son spent hours drawing a dice showing all six sides – very tricky! Another common choice is to draw people with clothes on, and an outline of the body underneath. It turns out that children find it much harder to draw what they see than what they know to be true.

The Six-Year-Old

- Most schools promote music and have instruments to play. Children can become fascinated by the range of noises and almost tunes they can produce. For some, music can be a great way to express emotions. Others approach it more in the manner of an explorer, trying out different instruments. By the end of their first year at school, a third of children think of themselves as musicians, and if you can succeed in encouraging your child and even provide some lessons, she may become one of the two per cent who regard themselves as being 'in training'.
- Your six-year-old is getting very good at drawing, and what she draws is now beginning to look true to life.

The Seven-Year-Old

- At last your child is able to think about perspective, and attempt to draw what she sees – especially if she is encouraged by you drawing, too! Copying someone else may help her find out about different techniques.

Perspective drawings, tuneful singing and skilful playing of musical instruments require hard work and many years of practice, but if your child is enthusiastic at seven, she may continue to be enthusiastic for life.

Drawing and music are windows into your child's soul, and it is immensely pleasurable for anybody who can immerse themselves unselfconsciously in an act that seems almost god-like – making something out of nothing.

Richard speaks

Richard, one of the *Child of Our Time* parents, is a professional artist and has earnt his living through art for sixteen years.

> ❝ *I do remember the first time I managed to capture a likeness myself when I did a drawing and I thought, 'Oh, I can actually draw that.' It started a fascination that grew very rapidly. Painting is an experience which is so positive, so pleasurable and your mind is just deliriously happy. At times it's been extremely difficult to make a living, but when you hit those pleasure moments you realize that at least there is something in your life that works really well for you.* ❞

The pleasure we get from making something is not just technical, it is also personal. Even adults draw different things when asked to make a simple picture – ample evidence that, for most of us, drawing is as much a reflection of what we think as what we see.

The technical and interpretative aspects of music and art are vital for everyone, but art and music become great through creativity, which is the power of self-expression coupled with the courage to break rules. Since children copy their parents, adults who want to nurture their child's natural creativity need to be creative themselves, abandoning their own correctness as often as possible for something wilder. Humour, incongruity, arbitrariness, provocation and unpredictability lead to lateral thinking.

DO IT YOURSELF

Test your family's creativity! Get a cardboard tube, for instance a kitchen-towel roll or a long poster tube. Give yourself three minutes to come up with as many imaginary uses for the tube as you can. Don't write them down – it takes too long – just make a mark on a piece of paper for each idea. You can count them up at the end. Then do the same test with your child – she may well be more creative than you!

The *Child of Our Time* families did this test, based on the Torrance Tests, too. Our adults and our six-year-old children had very similar average scores, but the spread was enormous, with one child stalling at seven ideas while the most prolific adult got twenty-five.

DON'T READ ON UNTIL YOU HAVE TESTED YOURSELF

The ideas from our contributors were wonderfully imaginative. Here are some of the adults' ideas:

A light sabre, a limbo-dancing pole, a hat stand, a contraption to blow bubbles in coffee, a hearing aid, quartered into legs for a table, folded to make a pair of bunny ears, a hammer, cut into short sections to make pots for growing sweet peas, a hiding place for secret messages, a workout machine and silent wind chimes.

And here are some of the children's ideas:

A tennis racket, a sausage, a sword, a baseball bat, a roller, an umbrella, a telescope, a chimney, a gun and a broomstick.

Not only do art and music have technical and creative aspects, they also have an emotional impact. Art in life – stunning views and beautiful pictures – can make the heart sing, but for many, music is key because music regulates emotion so effectively. Shops use music to sway their customers: classical melodies bestow an upmarket tone that helps justify high prices, while the mild musak in supermarkets is designed to keep you in the shop. Soft, slow music is calming, minor tones are sad, while fast rhythmic dance music revs us up.

A fascinating fact about the emotional effects of music

The best music has emotion at its core as well as technical virtuosity, and while some of our reactions to music are due to associations, others are purely biological. The heart is a responsive organ – as we all know! – and is especially sympathetic to music. So much so that it adjusts its rhythm to match the music we listen to. Fast rhythms elevate the heart rate, increase the speed of walking and generally energize us. Adults are often reticent dancers and so may not get the full benefit, but children have no such inhibitions and may dance to fast, beating music till they drop in a pile of giggles.

Experts believe that music is also good for the brain, increasing physical activity, speeding up the learning of language, and even maximizing your child's ability to do sums. Certainly musicians tend to be better than average at maths.

WHAT YOU CAN DO ... for all children

- Paint and make music yourself! Seeing how you value the activity – whether you are good or bad – will encourage your child because she loves to copy you. Giving her Bach symphonies or Van Gogh prints will help although they may be difficult, but if you work alongside her she'll work out what she can attempt for herself. Copying adults' behaviour is always helpful, as Suzuki has so brilliantly proved with his violin-playing youngsters.

- If you want your household to be creative – let yourself go! Fill your house with sound and beauty created by the whole family. Your child will love to play music and dance, to use colour and shape to make wonderful patterns and to be as creative as anything. Artistic and musical ability is open to virtually anyone and is enormously enhanced by experience and the freedom to choose.

WHAT YOU CAN DO ... for babies

- The language of music is easily understood and your baby already has her own musical preferences, and will love to be consulted. Watch her react to clapping, drumming, singing, dancing and nursery rhymes, see whether she likes her music soft or loud and tailor it to her enjoyment.

- Your baby is also fascinated by the things she sees and has a natural sense of beauty. You can tell what she likes best – black and white and shiny mobiles, sunny days with dappled light, whole trees and single leaves, insects, birds and animals that move, and, of course, her family.

- She is also naturally creative, experimenting with everything she encounters, which makes her ready to appreciate the world and to be appreciated in her turn.

WHAT YOU CAN DO ... for toddlers

- Your child is well able to use her fresh eyes to look, think, visualize and remember. She can see how things really are and learn how to work creatively to build likenesses out of colourful materials such as chalk, tin foil, patterned wrapping paper, fabric and bricks. She has untutored ears but will now use her growing coordination to make her own music, using spoons and saucepans, wood and metal, musical instruments and, of course, her own voice. Give her plenty of help and she'll make you some wonderful creations.

WHAT YOU CAN DO ... for older children

- Your child is endlessly curious and a natural artist. These are gifts to be cherished. So, what to do? This time it's all about detail. Scrutinize pictures with her to see precisely how they are made and show her how to copy them. Help her distinguish between what she sees and what she knows to be true but can't see, by giving her a camera and examining what is visible and what is occluded. Encourage her to draw on her emotions both in making and experiencing pictures, music and song, and give her challenges. A wonderfully creative person, Edward de Bono, asked children to draw machines that would variously stop cats fighting dogs, weigh an elephant and improve the human body. The children came up with extraordinary, original solutions.
- Nowadays there are plenty of galleries, museums, libraries and events offering your child opportunities to meet artists, musicians, story-tellers and dancers. You can follow up with ideas for your own kids' events – plays, exhibitions, music parties – however disorganized and discordant! All this, combined with your child's magnificent creativity, will help turn her into a real artist and add immeasurably to her happiness.

The power of words, numbers and the arts cannot be underestimated. Seeing, listening, making pictures and noises are instinctive and enrich us with intellectual challenges and emotional experiences. Without them, we wouldn't be human. And without other people to help us learn, we would be really stupid! Intelligence doesn't arise by accident; it is nurtured by all the wonderful people around us.

ZOË'S STORY

Zoë was a nervous little girl whose family liked to travel and took holidays in many different countries. Neither of her parents could speak any language other than English, but Zoë's mother always made sure she learnt enough words to find the right train and pay bills. One year, seven-year-old Zoë listened to her mother as she talked with the hotel manager and, remembering all those other holidays, said proudly, 'Mummy, you can speak all the languages in the world!' By the time she was older and Zoë realized how little her mother actually knew, she had already come to believe that languages were easy – and went on to become a linguist! Copying your parents is the most natural way to acquire the skills of language, maths, art and music.

So how does schooling help this natural process? And how much can teachers inspire their charges to want to learn, when they have to get them through educational hoops? Teachers are judged very largely by how quickly they can get children to read and write and do maths, and how obedient and quiet the class is. In the next part I shall look at the benefits and constraints of pre-school and school, and examine how your child can flourish in what is initially a weird and alien environment.

PART FIVE:
RULES FOR
SCHOOL

'Education is not the filling of a pail but the lighting of a fire.'

William Butler Yeats

A great school, coupled with enthusiastic parents, can ignite a passion for knowledge in your child that lasts for ever. And fuelling that passion is now more important than ever. Huge changes in work patterns and the rapid development of technology mean that anyone who can't move on gets left behind. So what do the best schools do to help? And how can your child fit in happily in the context of an increasing number of tests and exams?

JAMES'S STORY

James was born in 2000 on a tough London estate. His mother, Carol, has an enduring and endearing optimism and always wanted James and his sister Bernie to have a different life, to grow up clever and happy. But it has never been easy. Carol herself had very little education and when she was eleven her mum died and she and her brother went into care.

Having a family of her own was always going to be a challenge. When James was young, Carol broke up with his dad. Her next partner was violent, stole some possessions from Carol's flat when they were out and then kidnapped James, who was found hours later, badly frightened, after a police search. Carol was moved to a safe house.

So how did this troubled start affect James? Carol told us that, at home, James was wild and rebellious. But when he was three he went to pre-school. Pre-school was different.

At first James found it difficult. His teacher, Valerie, wasn't impressed either. She said that he was a handful who had to be watched. So what happened next seemed miraculous. James changed. He started to concentrate, became more sociable and, best of all, he was happy. His whole attitude transformed. Four months after he started, we visited again. 'I'm very pleased with him,' Valerie said with a big smile. 'The other kids like James, too, he's one of the nice bad boys – funny how people always admire them!'

But the change wasn't a miracle; James simply had brilliant teachers, the best I have ever met, and he was lucky, being just the right age to be given one of the government's new Sure Start pre-school places. So Valerie and the team became James's salvation, the school his safe haven.

But could it last? Spool on three years. After another move, James, now six, lives on another South London estate where three-quarters of the families are on benefit and crime has gone up by 20 per cent in the last year. It is a place where cognitive and behavioural scores of three-year-olds are frighteningly low. The ambiance has taken its toll and Carol is pessimistic about his future: 'I don't think James could be a doctor or a lawyer or anything high like that. I could be wrong but I think he'll stay at home and just sit, watch telly and play games.' So what does James think? 'I want to be a robber,' he says.

But James is still at a very good school with dedicated teachers who are much more positive. He's on a par with the rest of the class and is expected to work and behave well. He responds to praise and told us proudly that he has seven good-work stickers. And although he feels he isn't good at anything, his mother is proud of him and has learnt to tell him so. High-quality teaching from pre-school to primary school can make a huge difference long term. Teachers have power. Good teachers teach children to love school, and, more, to love learning.

There is an old adage, 'It takes a village to bring up a child.' James's village has many characters, but he's lucky with the most important: his teachers and his loving, cheerful mother.

There are few milestones that are as crucial and daunting in life as starting school, and the memory can stay with us for ever. We have to find our way round mysterious places; we must share territory with other bigger children; we have to deal for the first time with a strange adult who has as much power over us as our parents – our teacher. School is the first place where we realize we can fail publicly; and failure at school can have as lasting an effect as success.

This section is about how to prepare your child for the magic of school life – and its horrors. In Chapter Twenty-three I'm going to look at schooling from the age of five to the first tests at seven, and examine what your child needs intellectually and emotionally if he's to get a good start. But first, pre-school, where settling in is only easy if your child gets great teachers and has the basics – good manners, tolerance, listening and speaking skills. During this time he'll be preparing for the next challenge – school. Is he ready? I'll show you how to find out.

Home and Away

Pre-school is a new, confusing world. Your child needs to love his teachers if he's going to love school, and that's more likely to happen if home life has prepared him.

Going to school at four, rising five can be a huge shock if home life is very unstructured. That's where pre-school comes in. Pre-school is an intermediate stage and children from three to five can benefit. If done well, the combination of impressive home learning and excellent pre-school is dynamite. Children who get both will still be doing better at school ten years later and are not likely to stop! There has been a great deal of work done on what parents can do to help their pre-school child settle in, and you don't have to be rich to be good at it.

The power of the home-learning environment has been very well researched by an impressive group of British educationalists at London's Institute of Education. They call their research the EPPE (effective provision of pre-school education) project. They found that the most important things done by parents whose children do very well at pre-school last into primary school and beyond. These children have:

- A regular bedtime
- Rules about watching TV/videos
- Time to play with friends at home and in the park
- Outings, like shopping, with you
- Visits to relatives' and friends' houses
- Mealtimes where all the family sits down and eats good food together
- Time to read aloud and look at books
- Trips to the library, museums and parks
- Space to play with and talk about letters and numbers
- Opportunities to paint and draw at home
- Sing-songs with music, nursery rhymes and poems
- Responsibility for doing appropriate jobs around the house
- Help with making friends and learning to be considerate of others
- Resilience, concentration and persistence (see p.98 for tips).

Ideally, all of the above would be done some of the time. But if you're short on time then my friend Sian Williams, a pre-school specialist employed UNICEF – and, incidentally, a very wise person – has boiled the most important elements down to a five-point plan, which she showed me last year. It's being used in many parts of the world.

Children who go to pre-school – be it at three or four – generally get a better start, but not always. In education, as in anything else, there is the good and the bad, and the EPPE project uncovered a problem: some pre-schools are so bad the children do worse than if they hadn't gone at all. The key to all good pre-schools lies with the staff. If you have good, well-qualified teachers on board, all is likely to go a lot better than if the staff are less qualified. Your child is worth a great education in a happy environment, so don't let him down!

What to Look for in a Pre-School or Nursery

- The children are purposefully engaged and happy.
- The staff interact warmly and positively with the children.
- The children initiate interaction with the staff as much as the other way round.
- The nursery looks cheerful, organized and well cared for, and everything is accessible from your child's height.
- There is a code of behaviour that staff and children adhere to.
- Staff are interested in social development as well as educational aims.
- Staff are interested in your child's home environment.
- Each child is treated as a welcome individual.
- Most of the staff have qualifications and there is at least one qualified teacher.
- Staff observe the children and know when to get involved and when to leave them alone.
- There is time for shared thinking, when your child works

through a problem or a story with an adult.
- The teachers are willing to introduce anxious children slowly, keeping them by their side until they are ready to go.
- Parents are welcome, both in the mornings to help settle their children, and as helpers in the classroom.
- And finally, take your child to see the pre-school too. Look at how he behaves and ask yourself if you can imagine him being happy there.

You can learn a lot about a school by talking to staff, and as much again by talking to parents with children at the school.

Even with all this information, going to pre-school can be difficult. There are many reasons for this, but one is that your child might not know some really basic things, things that are so obvious they have been completely overlooked.

YOTA'S STORY

Yota was a lively girl at home, full of questions and interested in everything. Her mother, Shauna, was very proud of Yota, as were her grandparents, who were more than happy to look after Yota at their house while Shauna was out at work and provide the evening meal, after which they watched TV until it was time for Shauna to take Yota home to bed. Shauna, a single parent, had a job that bored her, but she wanted the best for her lively daughter and at the weekend they went shopping together, buying clothes and toys. This contented routine continued until Yota was four, when, quite suddenly, Shauna's father had a stroke. Yota was sent to pre-school and a paid childminder looked after her while Shauna was at work.

And Yota hated it. She went from being a talkative, smiley child to an angry and silent one, seeming happy only at weekends. Shauna wanted to find out what was wrong, so one morning she went to the pre-school and asked to see a teacher. Eventually a young woman appeared and ushered Shauna to a couple of chairs in a corridor, where Shauna explained how unhappy Yota was. The nursery helper – for she was not a teacher – tried to be patient, but had no real understanding of the problem and repeated that Yota was a quiet child, who didn't get into trouble. Questioned further, the young woman said she thought Yota was below average intelligence, but, she shrugged, 'There are lots like that round here.' Shauna was horrified. Surely the pre-school could offer more than just a shrug?

That afternoon Shauna had tea with Yota's childminder, an intelligent woman who worked part time at the local primary school. She told Shauna that the largely untrained teachers at the pre-school weren't very good about introducing children to the three Rs if they hadn't already been taught at home. Shauna was outraged; nevertheless, mulling it over, she came to the conclusion that she needed to do something – but what? Both the childminder and the nursery helper had talked about books, so Shauna went to the library for the first time.

Over the next few weeks, Shauna taught Yota that the wiggly lines in books have meaning, that Mummy knew which bus to take because she could see the number and which packet of cereal to buy because of the name on it. The books also showed Yota that language is made up of discrete words, which cleared up a mystery, for Yota, like many children, didn't know this. And finally, Shauna encouraged Yota to discover new words and concepts from the illustrated hardbacks they took out of the library every week.

Six months later, Yota and Shauna were still reading together, and Yota was at primary school. And this time she went well primed and settled in perfectly.

A fascinating fact about words

Once children reach pre-school and reception class, they rarely ask the meaning of words in stories. That's because in speech words often run on without any space between them, making it impossible to hear the distinction between a word and the one before or after it. Words will only become clearly separated in your child's mind when he learns to read; only then is the distance between each word made clear with a space.

All children need to find out about reading and numbers if they are to find pre-school easy, but the things they need to know aren't always well taught, particularly if the staff don't include trained teachers. Another big issue for small children is how to answer questions. Often they find adult questions completely impenetrable.

Alice and Mabel (aged three and three-quarters) speak

Adult: Who did you play with at school?
Alice: Toys.
Adult: Who did you play with?
Alice: Plasticine.

Adult: Can you tell me what you did at nursery?
Mabel: I don't want a boyfriend.
Adult: Did you see your boyfriend?
Mabel: No, don't want a boyfriend. I got Lucy.
Adult: You've got a good friend called Lucy?
Mabel: Yeah.
Adult: What do you enjoy doing with Lucy?
Mabel: Lucy's got homework.
Adult: And what do you enjoy doing with Lucy, what do you enjoy playing?
Mabel: I'm going to … I'm going to be a tiger.

I've witnessed hundreds of conversations like this and am sure that both Mabel and Alice thought their replies perfectly logical, but the adult here sounds a bit annoyed – it's certainly not logical to her!

Young children find it especially hard to answer adult questions if they are unrelated to what they are doing at the time. But the same children ask plenty of questions of their own when they are interested, so it's not questions that are the problem, it's the interpretation. As experience shows, young children attend not to what words mean, but to what people mean.

A fascinating fact about what children really want to know

Words are not nearly as interesting as the drama intrinsic to phrases and stories. So you will notice that your young child is less likely to discuss words even if he knows he's missed something. Sensibly, perhaps, he immerses himself in the story itself and wants to know important things like 'Why did that person hit him?', 'What happened next?' and 'What did his mummy say when he spilt the tadpoles?' When you look at the momentous importance of questions like that, bothering with individual words seems quite unnecessary.

When he is nearly five, your child will leave pre-school – or home – to go to school, where the rules are stricter and expectations higher. So how do you know if your child is ready to move? There are plenty of tests for what is called 'school readiness'. They usually focus on skills such as whether your child knows the names of colours, can copy simple shapes and cut out neatly. Some also examine early writing skills, such as whether your child can write all or part of his name or count up to ten. Others include day-to-day activities such as whether your child can dress himself, fasten up his shoes, hop, skip and jump. But there are other skills your child will need. One is the confidence to experiment, which we tested with the *Child of Our Time* children:

A DAY IN THE LAB

To be ready for school, it helps to be intellectually self-confident. We tried a very simple experiment with the *Child of Our Time* children when they were four years old. It involved a pair of scissors and three straws. All the children had to do was make a square.

Some children struggled, because they felt unable to damage the straws. Others didn't think to use the scissors at all. But the majority of

our children cut the straws to make four equal pieces which they put together to make a square. They had the ability to take an intellectual risk to solve a new problem, a useful attribute for success at school.

Children struggle to make a square out of three straws.

WHAT YOU CAN DO ... for your pre-school child

- Your child is going at his own pace. Some will get there fast, others lag behind. If your child seems slow it's rarely because he's stupid. He's not! He's just doing things in his own time. But if he is unhappy or anxious you may need to boost his confidence and foster his motivation using the techniques on pp.69–70. At pre-school, as later in life, confidence and motivation go a very long way.
- Great books, funny books, beautiful books – your child can't get enough of them. As you read, stop sometimes to see what he makes of the story and whether he understands all the words. Talking about words, not just with them, will give him a heightened understanding of language and prepare him for the next stage – reading to himself.
- There is no need for a child to learn to read or do sums before school; in many countries these skills are not taught formally until the age of seven. But though neither is likely to feature very strongly in your child's pre-school, a love of books and sense of number will help your child enormously as he settles into school. Some children arrive at the reception class not knowing about words; others, who have spent all their early childhood playing with objects and not books, may not appreciate the value of thinking about things that are not 'real'. Feeding your child's imagination, extending his language and making him aware of numbers will help his transition into school.

School at Last

'School days, I believe, are the unhappiest in the whole span of human existence. They are full of dull, unintelligible tasks, new and unpleasant orders and brutal violations of common sense and common decency.'

H. L. Mencken

Let's hope our children don't feel like H. L. Mencken, because they face more schooling than ever before. Fifteen thousand hours at school and five thousand homework hours are already the norm, and expectations are still rising. And then there are exams. Children now face about a hundred exams during their school career. So it is important to find a school your child will be comfortable in, with good but not pushy academic aspirations and plenty of non-academic activities, including sport, art and music.

Choosing a School

You won't necessarily get much of a choice of school – your local ones will always be the natural next step, but it is still worth checking them out. Do look back at the pre-school list in the previous chapter – lots of the ideas there are still appropriate – but there are also some extra issues to think about:

- Going round the school, you should sense an atmosphere of calm contentment, a hum of activity that is not too quiet and not too loud.
- You should see children doing responsible jobs, like taking the register back to the office.
- If you are going around with the head or the deputy, observe whether they know the children and say hello by name. This is polite and meshes in with the policy of mutual respect that good schools observe.
- Read the school's prospectus and code of behaviour and talk about how these are put into practice. Some schools tend to be more punitive than others, some more supportive. Do also ask about bullying. All schools have bullies, the issue is how the teachers deal with it.
- Check the turnover of teachers – it can be an indicator of school stability and happiness.

- You can see how the children interact if you have time to watch them at lunch or in the playground.
- Read the latest inspection report – the school should be able to give you a copy, otherwise look it up on the internet or ask the local authority or the inspectorate. This will tell you the schools' strengths and weaknesses and enable you to work out what support you may need to provide at home.

When your child walks into her reception class on the first day, she'll feel a strange combination of emotions. Exhilaration will be mixed with fear, and she'll be conscious of being both the youngest in the school and at the same time grown up in her new uniform.

DO IT YOURSELF

We gave our BBC TV audience a questionnaire to find out what they thought were the best tactics for their children as they start school. Here it is:

1 What's really going to make a difference to a child's school career?

a Mother's education

b Family income

c Private education

2 What do you say on the first day? Remember your child is just five.

a 'I want you to be good and do what the teacher tells you. So will you do that?'

b 'Your mum and I expect you to work hard. You've got to learn lots at school, that's the point of going there. OK?'

c 'You know Daddy and I did really well at school and we want you to do just as well as we did so you can get on in life. Can you try to do that?'

3 What can you do to get your child off to a good start?

a Encourage her to develop a vivid imagination and good ideas

b Make sure she looks good

c Make sure she has lots of interests she can pursue

4 Your child is doing well, but how could you help her do better?

a Find out about school by asking her about her day

b Make sure she doesn't eat junk food

c Talk with her about anything she wants

5 As the term progresses what should you say to keep her motivated?

a Keep praising her

b Only praise when she's done well

c Only praise when she's made an effort

Answers

1a Mother's education correlates much better with educational success than either of the others, perhaps because highly educated mothers home-educate, have high expectations and pass on practical tips for school.

2b If you want your child to learn, tell her so! If you just ask your child to be good she may become cautious, shy of asking questions in case she incurs the teacher's wrath. And children who are expected to do as well as a parent or a sibling usually ignore the advice partly because it is de-motivating to be compared to someone else; it's better to be encouraged for themselves.

3b The right answer is to look good. It's all very unfair, but there is no doubt that being physically attractive is a bonus for anyone. Having hobbies and a vivid imagination may be interesting, but at first people tend to judge by appearance. On the positive side, a friendly, humorous face is often more beautiful than a grumpy, disdainful one!

4c The right answer is to talk about anything and everything. Children often clam up when questioned; they prefer to take the lead and will tell you more if you listen well. Junk food is not good for a child, but avoiding it isn't as important as talking.

5c Praising a child for her effort encourages her to work, and to enjoy it. Constant praise may come to seem empty, and praising her only when she's done well may make her feel she's not allowed to fail.

School-based learning relies on knowing how to think in the 'right' way. You are allowed to make a mess with paints at school because it's set up that way, unlike at home. You have a wide choice of things to do and can often choose more freely than at home. These are freedoms for a child. But there is a skill that is often forgotten in preparing children for academic life and that is the art of answering questions. Your child started learning how to do that in pre-school and is quite capable of answering questions such as 'Do you want an ice-cream?' or 'What can you see in the picture?' But what happens if she is asked real school-style questions?

Children answering questions can be logical, creative, embarrassed, even frightened, but they are not slaves to the conventions – yet!

Some teachers have a terrifying habit of shooting out questions that require the 'right' answer. Preparing your child to answer questions such as 'What does a fish do differently from a person?' is difficult even if she is looking at a picture of a fish, but if she is to have a successful school career she needs to know how to deconstruct these sorts of questions. Some children even ask the teacher to clarify – definitely a good tactic! But there is more to this than meets the eye. Children don't get answers wrong accidentally.

Maggie, Ashok and Brady speak

Young children are often asked questions at school. Here are some of their answers.

Question: Which is the odd one out – an apple, an orange or a canary?
The right answer: the canary.

Maggie: Apple! Because it is the only green one!

Question: Where do you live?
The right answer: the town or the street

Ashok *(as if the question was ridiculous)*: My house.

Question: What's the capital of England?
The right answer: London

Brady *(fidgeting, knowing he was wrong)*:
My home! My home!

Question: What does this little girl want?
Illustration: child holding hand up for ice-cream
The right answer: An ice-cream.

Brady *(nearly crying)*: He wants his Mummy.

PROFESSOR MARGARET DONALDSON'S STORY

Margaret Donaldson was a remarkable psychologist with a great affinity for children. She knew that asking questions of children is not the best way to find out how much they know.

She was also an admirer of the great researcher Jean Piaget, the man who first mapped out children's intellectual development scientifically (see p.47). Children, he realized, develop their understanding of the world through trial, error and rigorous logic. Piaget finished his monumental work in the 1970s, but wonderful experimenters like Donaldson took his ground-breaking experiments and examined them even more closely.

One of these is Piaget's simple experiment on length. He got two same-length pieces of wood and laid them down like this:

Then he asked children if they were the same length.

Children above the age of about four said 'yes'.

Then he asked the children to watch what he was doing, and shifted the pieces of wood so they looked like this:

Now he asked the children 'Are they the same length?'

Children under seven commonly said 'no'.

Piaget deduced that this was because young children can't consider length independent from position. But was he right?

Margaret Donaldson did the test again, but discussed the answers carefully with the children themselves. She discovered that they may have known that the lines are the same length, but they also had other ideas to pursue. It turns out that children pay more attention to their own thoughts and less to slavishly follow-ing the adult route where only one answer can be right. This is what results:

1 Some children say the length must have changed because they ask themselves 'What does this adult *really* want?' and fathom out that the experimenter wouldn't have bothered to ask the question if the answer was 'yes'.

2 Others take the bold decision that, for them, the important aspect of the problem is not the absolute length of
the line but the fact that the second one goes further
along the page.

3 And some of the children are so interested by the move
that they decide to disregard the specific question in their
desire to look at the situation. The answer 'yes' is just a
holding position to give themselves time to think about
what shifting the line actually means.

How easy it is for your child to get muddled at school
over things that require particular types of answer and
don't allow for the deep thinking she does so well! At
school children are keen to please, so getting answers
to these sorts of questions 'wrong' can end up de-motivating them and even damaging their natural curiosity.

Children who are perfectly intelligent can be caught out because of
the distance between the real-life shifting situations that they are
used to at home, and the seemingly random abstractions required
for school. But being good at knowing the right answer is extremely useful at school, however antagonistic it can be to the joys of
creativity and imagination.

In order to be able to think about the 'right' answer, children need
to become more aware of other people's thinking, learning what aspects of a situation to attend to and what to safely ignore. This is
where support from home comes in. By talking about questions and
answers and learning particular facts, your child will become more
confident in answering. This is particularly important when it comes
to tests, which start very early in school and go on until you leave.
Early tests are often fundamentally about intelligence.

A fascinating fact about IQ

However intelligent you are, it is very likely that your child will
have a higher IQ than you! IQ has gone up by about ten points
a generation since it was invented at the end of the nineteenth
century, and new tests have to be brought out every so often
to reflect this. It may be because our diet has improved and
our culture grown more complex, but whatever the reason, we
have become more sophisticated at the type of problem-solving

required by IQ tests. There may be a particularly huge leap since the advent of computers and computer games, which require speedy reactions from players and the ability to analyse what is going on in several different places at once.

Of course, we do not have single but multiple intelligences. Everyone knows it is possible to be good at reading and hopeless at maths, and your child will already be developing her own focus. The best schools will notice this and put children in individual groups where they can each get what they need.

Learning about other people's thinking is also important if you are to be happy. Once at school, your child is likely to be very influenced by her peers, as we found with the *Child of Our Time* children when they were six.

Alison Lapper speaks

" *My son, Parys, used to wear nail varnish and now he won't wear it at all – he says all his friends will laugh at him. Parys doesn't like to wear jewellery any more and he won't touch brown bread. All his friends have white bread, so he has to too. When they start going to school a lot of their individuality disappears and I find it sad that he's had to conform at such a young age. He's six – give him a break!* **"**

The influence of peers will only get stronger as time goes on. One researcher found that while on average 30 per cent of school achievement is down to home life when a child is seven (and a lot of the rest is down to genetics), it drops to 27 per cent at eleven, and achievement in sixteen-year-olds is mostly due to school life, with parental influence trailing at just 14 per cent. In some situations, peer pressure can make even seven-year-old children take very odd decisions!

A DAY IN THE LAB

Last year we did an interesting test devised in the 1950s with the *Child of Our Time* children. The children were placed one by one with three little stooges, and the four were then asked to tell the experimenter which of three lines was the same length as the test line.

Such is the effect of peer pressure that nearly half of the *Child of Our Time* children gave the same – wrong – answer, copying the three stooges, even though it was obvious to a dispassionate observer which line was really the same length as the test line!

Peer pressure can lead to bad decisions but it is also a great motivator. Generally children join into groups of people like themselves and gain much-needed support. So here's just a short word about how to make friends, because friendship has a huge impact on how much your child will gain from school.

DO IT YOURSELF

How socially skilled is your child? Observe her trying to get what she wants and see if she uses some of these tried and tested techniques:

- Makes mutual eye contact.
- Sits with a friendly posture, oriented towards the other person.
- Smiles.
- Pays attention to the other person and looks interested.
- Responds to the other's non-verbal messages and reactions.
- Mirrors posture and facial expressions.
- Is willing to follow a conversational lead and take turns to speak.
- Makes animated gestures.
- Gets reasonably close.

  Everyone has their own style, and though shy children can take longer to deploy their strategies they are likely to be just as skilled when they relax.

Companions tend to boost school attainment because a happy child learns, while an unhappy child just longs to be somewhere else.

Such is the pressure on children to have a successful school career that there is probably not enough emphasis placed on making sure your child gets enough free time to think and imagine for herself. Some children respond by internalizing society's mores and start to drive themselves, some drop out of the race because they hate the pressure, but just a very few manage to achieve success without strain, simply by good planning …

CHARLIE'S STORY

Charlie was a merry six-year-old boy when I first realized he had an extraordinary talent for looking ahead. He had great social skills, but he didn't much like reading or maths, and he never stuck at any activity for very long. If there was something else that looked fun, he was there. Charlie's parents were highly educated and were not pleased to see him failing, but he was impervious to their ambitions and so sweet, they couldn't bring themselves to punish him.

But children always know what their parents need, and Charlie was no exception. He knew that if he fell far behind, they would make him have extra classes. This had already happened to his older sister and was, in his view, a waste of precious playtime. And he had his pride. He didn't like being at the bottom. Somewhere just below the middle was where he felt comfortable. Luckily Charlie was intelligent and a great planner.

By the time he was seven he had worked out how to get the grades he wanted. He did his maths homework on the kitchen table, his mum close by to help. Reading happened at bedtime and, if needed, he tapped into his father's love of information. And so, with a minimum amount of work, Charlie got just enough done to stay out of trouble.

Never one to waste a good idea, Charlie went on like this for the rest of his school career, checking with his teachers to find out if he had done enough and persuading his family to help. He left school at eighteen with top grades in all his subjects, and a good university place, without, he claimed, ever concentrating for longer than twenty minutes at a time.

If there is any under-rated skill your child needs to develop, it is the ability to organize herself. In our demanding and time-starved world, this one simple thing will make all the difference to her life. She'll feel in control, less stressed and able to free up time to do all the things she loves.

WHAT YOU CAN DO ... for your school-aged child

- Let your child know how much you value education and how certain you are that she will enjoy her years at school, though there will be good and bad! Prepare her carefully and talk about anything she likes when she comes home and she'll tell you all you need to know about her days.
- Read with her – it can never be said often enough! – play with her and make sure she has plenty of time to do what she wants. School can be exhausting, so time for mulling things over and playing out fantasies is now especially precious.
- By the time she is seven your child will probably be given some homework. This is a great opportunity for her to take responsibility. Let her plan the timetable and do the work herself. Don't take over and don't even monitor it closely. Why? Because homework is about her relationship with her teacher, not with you. If she does it by herself – asking for help if she needs it – she'll be proud. If she doesn't, her teacher will tell her off and she'll know to do it next time. Seven is a great time to start because it's when most children are keen to please and this liberates you to be a sympathetic facilitator rather than having to crack the whip. I know many families who have done this and never had problems with homework again!
- Be confident in your child; your belief in her will be hugely beneficial, especially when things are not going well. She is her own best teacher, already a great logician, mathematician and linguistic expert – and she loves you!

EPILOGUE

'I have found the best way to give advice to your children is to find out what they want and then advise them to do it.'

Harry S. Truman

Child of Our Time: Early Learning has explored the marvellous mechanics of your child's mind, starting with how children learn, each in their own way. We've seen how motivation fuels learning, memory stores it, the thinking brain uses it and, finally, how your child can get the best out of school. The things children learn in their early years will affect them for the rest of their lives and play a crucial role in the journey from childhood to a fulfilled adulthood.

Early learning has shaped us since Homo sapiens started to walk the earth. But the massive technological upheaval of the twenty-first century means that we now have to learn faster than ever before, mastering many new skills not just when we are young, but through-out our lives. Lifelong learning is no longer something that can be engineered and organized for children by teachers and parents. Now-adays we have to take responsibility for our own education.

A DAY IN THE LAB: A story about self-determination

Fifty years ago, a class of children were given a book by their teacher. Books were more precious then than now and they read theirs with great attention and enormous pleasure, knowing that their teacher had thought hard about which book would best suit each of them, and feeling honoured to be given a personal present.

Fifty years later the scenario was played out again. Children were given a book carefully chosen by their teacher, but the children were not impressed. Their teacher's book would, they said, be boring. In the room were other books wrapped in brown paper. The children decided to take one of those instead because they assumed that their blind choice would be better than their teacher's thoughtful one.

This extraordinary shift from belief in authority to rejection of it shows how much children expect to be able to decide for themselves.

This story underlines a major cultural shift. No longer do we auto-matically respect authority nor do we expect to obey orders blindly.

Instead, individuals like to be consulted not told, to be in control rather than merely dutiful.

Our children also expect respect and demand an increasing level of self-determination, something that can seem at odds with an education system based on conformity and exams. So is the determination of our children to do things their own way bad? No! Knowing that your child is his own person; allowing him to be responsible and find his way through difficulties is healthy. It is good to experiment, useful to learn by mistakes, wonderful to revel in success, and, above all, it is motivating to be trusted.

Learning early, learning things parents approve of, learning things they don't, learning because you want to and because you can. It's learning that makes us human.

BIBLIOGRAPHY

Acredolo, Linda and Goodwin, Susan, *Baby Minds: Brain-Building Games Your Baby Will Love*, Bantam Books, 2005.
> *Based on brain-development stages, this book showcases games that help you understand how your child thinks.*

Baddeley, Alan, *Your Memory: A User's Guide*, Pryon, 2002.
> *General book about memory; useful for you and your children!*

Brewer, Sarah and Cutting, Alex, *A Child's World*, Headline, 2001.
> *A unique insight into how children begin to work things out, from their first thoughts to teenage angst.*

Cole, Michael, Cole, Sheila and Lightfoot, Cynthia, *The Development of Children*, Worth Publishers, 2004.
> *Detailed textbook of child development, interesting for those of you who want a breadth of knowledge about children across the world.*

De Bono, Edward, *Children Solve Problems*, Penguin Books, 1972.
> *Children draw pictures to solve problems, such as how to stop a dog and a cat fighting, showing their creative and matter-of-fact sides.*

Dinkmeyer, Don Sr, McKay, Gary, Dinkmeyer, James, Dinkmeyer, Don Jr and McKay, Joyce, *Systematic Training for Effective Parenting of Children Under Six,* American Guidance Service, 1997.
> *Practical guide to understanding children's behaviour, designed to encourage cooperation and increase their self-esteem.*

Doherty-Sneddon, Gwyneth, *Children's Unspoken Language*, Jessica Kingsley Publishers, 2003.
> *How to interpret children's body language.*

Donaldson, Margaret, *Children's Minds*, Fontana Press, 1992.
> *How children think about language, numbers, reading and writing, and why they do – and don't – learn.*

Emler, Nicholas, *Self-Esteem: The Costs and Causes of Low Self-Worth*, Joseph Rowntree Foundation, 2001.
> *A detailed look at children's confidence levels.*

Faber, Adele and Mazlish, Elaine, *How to Talk So Kids Will Listen, and Listen So Kids Will Talk*, Avon Books, 1980.
> *A book to help you get your kids talking and listening with lots of practical examples.*

Gardner, Howard, *Multiple Intelligences: The Theory in Practice,* Basic Books, 1993.
> *The man who publicized multiple intelligences describes how they work in practice.*

Gopnick, Alison, Meltzoff, Andrew and Kuhl, Patricia, *How Babies Think: The Science of Childhood,* Weidenfeld & Nicolson, 1999.
Insight into babies' minds, how babies think and how they grow.
Hamer, Dean and Copeland, Peter, *Living with Our Genes: Why They Matter More Than You Think*, Macmillan, 1999.
Stories and analyses of the effects genes have on our personality.
Leach, Penelope, *Your Baby and Child: From Birth to Age Five*, Dorling Kindersley, 2003.
Authoritative all-round childcare from nappies to tantrums.
Levine, Mel, *A Mind at a Time: How Every Child Can Succeed*, Simon & Schuster, 2003.
A paediatrician describes how school-age children can deal with problems from concentration to memory and thinking.
Livingstone, Tessa, *Child of Our Time: How to Achieve the Best for Your Child from Conception to Five Years*, Bantam Press, 2005.
My first book is about how to win in the first five years, with ideas and help for those first tricky months of life, learning language, the terrible twos, and making friends at school.
Lloyd, Sue, *The Phonics Handbook: Jolly Learning*, 2nd edition, 1994.
How to teach reading, writing and spelling. Often used in schools.
Nunes, Terazhina and Bryant, Peter, *Children Doing Mathematics (Understanding Children's Worlds)*, Blackwell, 1996.
Maths taught and understood from the point of view of the child.
Oates, John and Grayson, Andrew, *Cognitive and Language Development in Children*, Blackwell Publishing Ltd in association with The Open University, 2004.
Written for students of child development, this is a clear and detailed book about how children learn.
Piaget, Jean, *The Language and Thought of the Child*, Routledge, 1959.
Piaget, Jean and Barbel, Inhelder, *The Psychology of the Child*, Routledge and Kegan Paul, 1973.
The grandfather of child psychology, Piaget observed his own children to find out how children learn to think and speak. Full of wonderful descriptions and extraordinary discoveries.
Skinner, Burhaus, *About Behaviourism*, Knopf, 1974.
The man who invented the science of behaviourism, and researched the effects of rewards and punishments on motivation, talks about his work.
Suzuki, Shinichi, *Ability Development from Age Zero* (Suzuki Method International), trans. Nagata, Mary Louise, Warner Bros Publication Inc., 1981.

Suzuki's own words about how to encourage happy learning, based on his work with music and his extensive experience with young children.

Tizard, Barbara and Hughes, Martin, **Young Children Learning** (2nd edition), Blackwell, 2002.

Insight into how young children understand their role at school, based on detailed observations of children from all walks of life at home and at school.

Ward, Sally, **Babytalk**, Random House, 2000.

Practical help for parents who want their children to learn to talk, especially if they seem to be falling behind.

Winston, Robert, **The Human Mind – And How to Make the Most of It**, Bantam Press, 2003.

Fascinating book about how we think – and how we got here.

WEBSITES

BBC Sites

www.bbc.co.uk/parenting

Best free website for lots of great stuff on kids, including advice on many subjects, some illustrated with film clips from several sources including Child of Our Time. The site has information about practically everything from toilet-training to health, literacy, behaviour, play and childcare. If you want to find out more about the TV series, search for 'Child of Our Time'.

www.open2.net/childofourtime

Try the Open University website for fun interactive tests linked with Child of Our Time, and for questionnaires, ideas for games and courses on child development.

www.bbc.co.uk/cbeebies and www.bbc.co.uk/cbbc

Website for the BBC's digital channel for kids under six, with programme information; games and competitions; print and colour; make and do; music and songs; and watching and listening.

UK Government Sites

www.standards.dfes.gov.uk

Primarily aimed at practitioners, 'Birth to Three Matters' (you can search for this on the site) is just one of several documents that provide information on child development, effective practice, examples of play *activities to promote play and learning, guidance on planning and resourcing, and meeting diverse needs.*

www.ioe.ac.uk/schools/ecpe/eppe

EPPE is a research project that finds out what is good and bad about pre-school education and has followed the educational fortunes of children from three to eleven. Once you get to the site, look for 'findings' and 'EPPE findings'. These give you a summary of research so far, and include the following useful document:

Sylva, K., Melhuish, E., Sammons, P., Siraj-Blatchford, I., Taggart, B. and Elliot, K., ***The Effective Provision of Pre-School Education (EPPE) Project: Findings from the Pre-school Period***, Department of Education and Skills, 2003.

Learning Sites

www.acceleratedlearning.com

Subscription site and online store with activity cards, guidebook and scores of games for pre-reading, writing and numeracy.

www.coe.uga.edu/torrance

Free site with creativity resources based on the work of a creative pioneer, Dr E. Paul Torrance.

www.literacytrust.co.uk

Free site about reading, writing and talking, including a wide range of research reports on subjects like the effects of television on language development.

www.familiesonline.co.uk

The website for Families *magazine provides reviews by real mums, a choice of features, listings of events, forums, plus pages of local information from local editors.*

www.allkindsofminds.org

All Kinds of Minds is a non-profit site that helps develop an alliance between parents, educators and children, offering learning challenges and activities that may help students minimize or overcome their differences in learning.

www.24hourmuseum.org.uk

Good interactive site and ideas for excursions in towns across the UK.

Special Sites

www.bda-dyslexia.org.uk

British Dyslexia Association.

www.dyspraxiafoundation.org.uk

Dyspraxia Foundation.

www.aboutdyscalculia.org and www.mathematicalbrain.com.
Two websites for people who have problems with maths.
www.addiss.co.uk
Attention Deficit Disorder Information and Support Service.
www.nas.org.uk
National Autistic Society, including information on autism and Asperger syndrome.

PERMISSIONS

Text Credits

p.22, Do It Yourself chart adapted from Colin Rose, *Accelerated Learning*, 1987, www.acceleratedlearning.com

p.87, Self-esteem questionnaire, M. Rosenburg, *Society and the Adolescent Self-Image*, revised edn; Middletown, CT: Wesleyan University Press, 1989.

p.162, extract from Ogden Nash, 'Put Back Those Whiskers I Know You', Good Intentions, 1942. Reproduced in *Candy Is Dandy*. Copyright as in US edition.

Picture Credits

Except for the images mentioned below, all photos were kindly supplied by the author and her friends, and various mums, dads, uncles, aunts and family friends at Transworld. Stills from the BBC series *Child of our Time* appear on pp. 12, 24, 25, 26, 34, 37, 42 (top), 104/05, 115, 120, 166/7, 171, 173, 186 and 229; the BBC also kindly supplied the images on pp. 3, 13, 42 (bottom), 89, 92, 121, 122, 179, 184 and 238.

Other images are credited as follows:

Corbis: 10/11 (© Rune Hellestad), 48 (© Vincent Mo/zefa), 65 (© Kevin Dodge), 96 (© Awilli/zefa), 134 (© Poppy Berry/ zefa), 216 (© Paul Hardy); **Alamy**: 23 (© Charles Mistral), 36 (© Bubbles Photo Library), 40 (© Image State), 67 (© Edward Bock), 77 (© blickwinkel), 113 (© Martin Harvey), 196 (© Bubbles Photo Library); **Rex Features**: 82 (Fotex); **Getty Images**: 95 (Tony Anderson).

ACKNOWLEDGEMENTS

This book would never have been written if it hadn't been for the television series *Child of Our Time*. It is one of the most extraordinary and fascinating projects in the television landscape, and I have been fortunate enough to work on it for the last eight years with a remarkably dedicated, versatile and talented group of people.

Child of Our Time would not be the project it is without Professor Robert Winston, friend and inspiration – I owe him a great debt. Creative Director Sarah Hargreaves has been at the heart of the series' epic journey since the very beginning. My thanks are also due to Glenwyn Benson and Emma Swain, who marshalled the resources of the BBC to give the project wings.

The *Child of Our Time* television team have been a tower of strength and created a legend of a series. All the gifted and intelligent series producers, producers, directors, coordinators, assistant producers, researchers and secretaries who have worked on the series through the years have contributed great things not just to the programmes, but indirectly to the book. My special thanks also go to Caroline Holland, Dinah Lord, Louise Bourner, Danuta Stanczyk and producer Sadie Holland, whose unfailing devotion to the series and generous input into the book has been very important.

I am very grateful to my wonderful agent, Maggie Pearlstine and her colleague Jamie Crawford for their unwavering support and encouragement, and, of course, to the excellent team at Bantam Press – Sally Gaminara, Kate Samano and Sheila Lee, who turn my manuscripts into cogent and beautiful pieces of work.

I would like to thank Siân Williams for insight, Charlie Jewell for patience, Zoë Jewell for passionate discussion, and Lisa Newman for keeping me sane. Our academic partners, John Oates and Professor David Messer of the Open University and Professor Heather Joshi from the Institute of Education have been immensely supportive, as have Judith Smyth and Aileen Buckton. I also owe an immense debt to all the psychologists, neurophysiologists, sociologists, doctors and parenting experts who have done the meticulous and inspiring research on which this book is based, some of whom are referenced in the bibliography. I hope they will enjoy the interpretation of their work and forgive the deficiencies.

And last but not least, I would like to thank the *Child of Our Time* families and all the others whose stories are woven into the book and whose children are utterly captivating.

INDEX

Polish language, 27

praise: effective, 116; motivation, 65; reward, 76–9

pre-school, 223–9: preparation for, 223–4; settling in, 220, 221; unsatisfactory, 224, 225–6; what to look for, 224–5; what you can do, 229

primacy effect, 129

punishment: physical, 112; praise and, 78, 79; strategy, 71; unfair, 78

Q

questions: adult, 226–8; teachers', 234; what children really want to know, 228

quizzes, 56

R

rats, 73, 74

reading, 188–92: database of words, 189; first words, 188–9; phonics, 188, 190–2; pre-school, 226; spellings, 190; stages, 184–5; teaching, 188

recognizing people, 18, 19

rehearsal, 124, 129

repetition, 143

resilience, 93–9; babies, 98; importance of, 223; nurturing, 116; older children, 99; tests, 95; toddlers, 98; traits, 96; what you can do, 98–9

responsibility, 64

rewards, 73–81; babies, 80; drawing experiment, 75–6; motivation, 73–4; older children, 81; praise, 76–9; strategy, 71; toddlers, 80; what you can do, 79–81

rhymes, 148, 194, 203

roads, crossing, 33

rote learning, 53–6: learning style, 31, 53; maths rules, 201; quizzes, 55–6; spelling, 193; things learned by rote, 54; TV, 54–5; use of, 123

routines, learning by association, 34

rules, 168, 170–1, 195, 200–1

S

scaffolding, 68–9, 176, 194

school, 231; choosing a school, 231–2; effects of, 220–1; peer pressure, 237–8; pre-school, 220–1, 223–9; questions asked at school, 234–6; school readiness, 228–9; tactics for starting school, 221, 232–3; what you can do, 240

self-belief, 83–91; babies, 91; fear of failure, 85; gender and self-esteem, 84; lack of, 64; learned helplessness, 86–7; older children, 91; toddlers, 91; what you can do, 90–1; worried parents, 88–9

self-determination, 243–4

self-esteem: test, 87–8; the unattractive student's story, 90

self-worth, lack of, 64

Seligman, Martin, 85–6

senses: memorizing with, 126–7; sensory learning styles, 24; *see also* hearing, looking, smelling, tasting, touching

serotonin, 94

sharing, 199, 200, 205

sign language, 180, *see also* gestures

Simons, Daniel, 132

singing: rote learning, 55–6; in tune, 211, 212

skills: fine motor, 184, 210; learning by association, 34; learning by visualization, 27; newborn baby's, 15–16; social, 26, 29, 238; transferable, 106

Skinner, B. F., 73, 74

smelling: baby's skills, 15; learning by association, 18, 35

smiling, 18

social: skills, 26, 238; style, 29

solitary style, 26, 29

Solity, Jonathan, 189, 200–1

songs, 54, 55–6, 194, 203, 210

speaking, 69–70

spelling, 54, 190, 192–3

stimulation, 162–3

stress inoculation, 93

Stroop Test, 104–5

Suzuki, Shinichi, 197–8

synaesthesia, 127–8

T

tactile learning style, 21, 23, 28
Tajet-Foxell, Britt, 43
Taliesen, 184
talking to your child, 65–6, 193–5
tasting, 15
teachers, 217, 220–1, 234
telephone numbers, 138, 148
testosterone, 202
thinking: basics, 165; deep thinking, 169; development of thinking power, 165–7; effects of exercise, 174–5; logical conclusions, 169; maintaining focus, 169–70; rules, 168, 170–2; strategies, 173; visualization, 81; what you can do, 176–7
time, 166
tools, 165
touching, 15, 17
tunes, 209, 212
TV, 42, 53, 54–5, 56, 112

U

unborn babies: response to numbers, 198; response to music, 33, 209: response to sound and light, 208

V

verbal working memory, 136

video: games, 105–6; setting date and time, 83
violence, 79
visual learning style, 21, 22, 23, 24, 27
visual working memory, 136
visualization: learning new skills, 27; memory aid, 148–50; multi-tasking, 136; power of, 28; remembering messages, 138; thinking, 81

W

Watson, John, 74
Williams, Sian, 223–4
winning, 63
word power, 179; accent, 182; babies, 194; big words, 185; child's first words, 18; gestures, 180, 183–4; language and newborns, 180; language checklist for two-year-olds, 185–6; language development, 181–8; meaning of words, 226; newborns, 180; older children, 195; pre-school, 226; reading and writing, 188–95; toddlers, 195; what you can do, 193–5; words in stories, 226
worried parents, 49–50, 88–9
writing, 184–5, 188, 192

Dr Tessa Livingstone has a Psychology and Physiology degree from Oxford and a PhD in Brain Sciences. After working with children in Europe and the Middle East, she has been making documentaries for the BBC for the past twenty years. Watching her own children Zoë and Charlie grow up focused Tessa's attention on children's psychology in the most graphic way and showed how fascinating, complex, precious, baffling and enjoyable children can be.

In 1998 Tessa started to create the BBC landmark television series *Child of Our Time*, which was conceived as a twenty-year longitudinal study of childhood. The project is designed to follow twenty-five children, born at the start of the millennium, as they grow up. The series has attracted a large following from viewers for whom the eclectic mix of science with absorbing human stories has been engaging, moving and inspiring. As the children move into their second decade, *Child of Our Time* will show how genes and environment combine to make us who we are.

Ten years after the series began, Tessa is now the Executive Producer and *Child of Our Time* is growing in scope and ambition, offering insight and parenting advice to millions of people across the world.